A Director's Guide

Financing growth

HELPING DIRECTORS TO FOSTER AND FINANCE BUSINESS EXPANSION

Editor, Director Publications: Tom Nash
Managing Editor: Lesley Shutte
Production Manager: Victoria Davies
Design: Halo Design
Commercial Director: Simon Seward
Managing Director: Andrew Main Wilson
Chairman: George Cox

Published for the Institute of Directors
and Grant Thornton
by Director Publications Ltd
116 Pall Mall London SW1Y 5ED

Editorial: 020 7766 8910
Production: 020 7766 8960
Sponsorship: 020 7766 8885
Copy sales: 020 7766 8766
Facsimile: 020 7766 8990

© Copyright November 1999
Director Publications Ltd

Price £9.95

YOURS TO HAVE AND TO HOLD
BUT NOT TO COPY

Director Publications Ltd   Kogan Page Ltd
116 Pall Mall   120 Pentonville Road
London SW1Y 5ED   London N1 9JN

© Director Publications Ltd 1999

British Library Cataloguing in Publication Data
A CIP record for this book is available from the British Library
ISBN 0 7494 3147 4

Printed and bound in Great Britain

Contents

Financing – facts and figures
Useful contacts

Whose business is this?
Mine or the taxman's?

Does it sometimes seem as if the person gaining most from your efforts is the taxman? ■ No one enjoys paying tax, but you can make the pain more bearable. Efficient tax management can provide excellent opportunities to help grow your business and reduce your tax burden. ■ At Grant Thornton we work with you to make sure tax-saving opportunities are identified. We can advise on the tax implications of funding, investments, acquisitions, buyouts, or any other aspect of commercial expansion. ■ And should you be unfortunate enough to face a random Inland Revenue investigation, our team of specialists will be at your side from day one. ■ To find out how we can help your business grow and develop, call us now on 020 7728 2758, e-mail melanie.tibbert@gtuk.com, visit our website at www.grant-thornton.co.uk, or return the reply-paid card opposite page 64.

Grant Thornton

Grant Thornton, the UK Member Firm of Grant Thornton International,
is authorised by the Institute of Chartered Accountants in England and Wales to carry on investment business

Finding the money

George Cox, Director General, Institute of Directors

Small and medium-sized enterprises (SMEs) have been the major engine for economic growth in Britain over the last 20 years, creating the majority of new jobs over this period and bringing increased competition, innovation and flexibility to the economy. As a result, it is now recognised by both government and economic commentators that the continued growth of smaller companies is essential to Britain's future prosperity.

Growth, however, needs to be fostered. As well as thorough planning, hard work, skill and flair, a vital ingredient is adequate finance. Despite the undoubted benefits that SMEs bring to the economy, they still suffer from difficulties in raising the money they need in order to invest, compete and expand.

Banking facilities for smaller companies – though much improved since the bloodbath of the early nineties recession – tend to be too inflexible. As for equity finance, small fast-growing enterprises, particularly in the high-tech sector, still perceive the existence of a so-called "equity gap", with City fund managers concentrating investment in large, quoted companies, while venture capitalists, despite their name, expect a high return for minimal risk.

Often smaller firms simply do not seek external finance, particularly equity finance, because they believe it is both time-consuming and very expensive to obtain and are unaware how best to acquire it. This clear, practical guide, written by expert authors, will help the directors of smaller companies to understand and overcome such obstacles.

IꝹD

THE
Chartered Director

Be recognised as a professional director

CHARTERED DIRECTOR

The IoD's Chartered Director initiative ensures directors' continued professional education and development.

CRITERIA

Admission to the profession of Chartered Director is open to all IoD members and Fellows with the requisite qualifications who are able to demonstrate the knowledge and experience required to become a member of the profession and who undertake to observe the IoD's Code of Professional Conduct.

BENEFITS

There are clear personal benefits to becoming a Chartered Director. They are recognised as directors:

■ *who have achieved standards of professional knowledge and experience;*

■ *who have made a serious commitment to their profession;*

■ *who have undertaken to act with probity and honesty.*

The letters *C.Dir* that Chartered Directors may append to their names are an easily recognisable badge of professionalism.

As a condition of continued registration, "chartered" members must commit to Continuing Professional Development (CPD) – at least 30 hours a year keeping themselves abreast of both practical and theoretical developments in direction.

To find out more about becoming a Chartered Director, telephone 020 7451 3210, or visit the IoD's web site at www.iod.co.uk

The IoD is ideally suited to help Chartered Directors achieve their Continuing Professional Development (CPD) requirement.

Look out for this symbol which is displayed on IoD products and publications that can assist directors in achieving their CPD requirement.

Improving the rate of survival

Tim Waterstone, founder Chairman of HMV Media Group

When explaining how growth can best be financed, one has to start from the position that the odds are against the survival of all small companies. Competition these days is so tough, and so global, and so ruthless in its application. Unless they are fortunate enough to be within a currently and, perhaps momentarily, fashionable sector – the Internet today, pharmaceuticals a generation back, once upon a time railroads – founders and owners of small businesses find the investment world stacked against them.

Banks and venture capital houses want size and they want growth. You can take the choice of staying small, and ignore the lot of them, and live off cash flow. But then the big players come along and cut you to ribbons, and you're gone.

The truth is that there is only one way for a small company to survive. And it is to have a laser-like accuracy of perception about the market it is in, and its own position and identity within that market, and the way that it can weave through the jungle to become one day a dominant player. Anyone can do it, but it requires courage, total clarity of vision and great powers of persuasiveness and leadership, and an instinctive understanding of what and when the financing hurdles are going to be and how they are to be negotiated.

Finally, what the developing company needs is self belief, the ability to convince investors and, above all, an intense, unbending desire to win.

I think the time is right to float on AIM...but how do I know for sure? Where can I turn to for impartial advice?

Determining whether your company should go public is probably one of the most significant decisions you will have to make. ■ At Grant Thornton we have an unrivalled understanding of the objectives and motivations of growing businesses and our many years' experience of working on flotations makes us ideally placed to offer advice. ■ We have strongly supported the Alternative Investment Market (AIM) from the outset and as a Nominated Adviser (NOMAD) have floated more than 25 companies onto AIM, making us one of the most active NOMADS in AIM. ■ Our experienced and knowledgeable partners and staff are keen to help aspiring and existing AIM companies alike. To find out how we can help your business, call us now on 020 7728 2758, e-mail melanie.tibbert@gtuk.com, visit our website at www.grant-thornton.co.uk, or return the reply-paid card opposite page 64.

Grant Thornton

Chapter 1

Why grow anyway?

In today's competitive marketplace, successful companies need to grow says Andrew Godfrey, head of growth and development services at Grant Thornton

It is universally agreed that small and medium-sized businesses (SMEs) form the linchpin of the UK's economy. Nevertheless, the characteristics of these businesses are as varied as those of their owners. What we do know is that most people running their own business face similar issues and share similar concerns, many of which revolve around management problems associated with the challenges of growth, raising finance or a combination of the two. How owners of SMEs respond depends to a great extent on their own personal priorities.

In Grant Thornton's *European Business Survey* we asked owners of SMEs about the extent to which their personal goals influence their business decisions. Four main categories or clusters emerged from the research, which provide an indication of the challenges that small and medium-sized business owners face if they are to achieve their ambitions:

- *The business-oriented (28 per cent): primarily their goal is to combine growth with control. They are also concerned about income and investment;*

- *The dynasts (32 per cent): their primary goal is to grow the business and pass it on to the next generation;*

- *The protectionists (22 per cent): their main priority is to keep their business at its present size while protecting their investment;*

- *The family-oriented (18 per cent): these are the owners of the traditional family business, whose goal is to keep the business at its current size and pass control on to the next generation.*

Within this book about financing growth we are primarily concerned with the first two clusters. However, the priorities of all companies change over time. A young entrepreneur who sets up a company with the aim of selling it within five years may subsequently develop a desire for his children to take over from him. Alternatively, a "sleepy" family-oriented company may be forced into growth by market conditions – "grow or die".

MOTIVATORS FOR GROWTH

Indeed in today's competitive marketplace, successful companies have to grow, if only to keep pace with their market's growth rate. All companies should be aiming to achieve some form of growth, not only to increase shareholder value, but because a dynamic environment is a primary motivator for attracting the best people to become involved with the business.

It is, in fact, very difficult to plan to stand still without going into decline. Without dynamism not only do shareholders' returns diminish in the short term, but low personal motivation throughout the organisation leads to a lack of innovation resulting in poor prospects for the long term as well.

Accordingly, every company needs to determine its growth prospects and have a clear strategy in place. As a business matures, it is necessary to regularly review both the company's objectives and those of its controlling shareholders. If these objectives are in harmony and focused to take account of the business environment, then the company's chances of success will be greatly increased.

IMPROVING RETURNS THROUGH MARKET DOMINANCE

Marketing strategy is the most important element of strategic management for small businesses, most of which find it difficult to influence their market. However, with growth, both the company's ability to influence the market and the market's awareness of the company accelerate. All other things being equal, growth and market dominance can then become self-perpetuating. (This is an ideal to which all companies aspire, but which few achieve.)

Market dominance enables companies that have become

larger and more sophisticated, or that offer a real niche service or product, to pick and choose which contracts to accept and which to turn away. Because they can attract better quality work at the right price – and, indeed, turn away lower quality work – their profitability is certain to increase. In addition, for companies enjoying this status the business risk of losing a key contract is reduced, thanks to market strength and the fact that the business is less reliant on any one customer.

Once market dominance has been achieved, the issues change. As well as seeking to achieve a position of market leadership, if a company is to grow effectively it must give regular consideration to diversification of its product/service offering and to the integration of new developments within the current structure.

ATTRACTING THE BEST PEOPLE

A dynamic and growing enterprise will be better positioned to attract dynamic executives whose motivation is to work within a vibrant organisation and who have the drive to move the business forward.

A growing business is also better placed to develop a remuneration policy that rewards executives according to performance. In particular, as the business continues to grow, awarding performance-related bonuses or providing equity will attract new executives, who may bring experience of working in much larger organisations. What's more, a company with a growth culture, whose executives benefit from a long-term reward package, is more likely to retain good people. There are, of course, downsides to providing executives with equity – such as diluting shareholdings and increasing the level of scrutiny from "outsiders". However, this can be overcome by reward structures designed to be equally attractive to new executives, such as phantom share schemes.

One of the greatest downsides to growth, as far as the owner-manager is concerned, is that it leads to the need for more employees and, therefore, an increasing number of staff-related distractions. In a small company, seemingly trivial problems are sometimes blown up out of all proportion: the cleaners haven't turned up,

Joe doesn't get on with Fred, John's office isn't big enough, Hilary gets paid less than Samantha. Accordingly, the company needs to develop a management structure that can deal with issues of this kind – one that will limit the owner-manager's exposure to them. However, he or she will never be completely absolved and needs to accept that this is the price one pays for growth.

RAISING FINANCE

Raising finance, particularly when you need it most, always appears to be a major hurdle. However, what will become apparent throughout the rest of this book is that, if a business is to secure any kind of equity funding, it must be able to demonstrate the potential for investors to obtain a return on their capital. The business also needs to be supported by a strong management team. Without these characteristics the likelihood of raising equity finance at any level is severely restricted.

Even if these criteria are met, there are more financing options available to larger companies than to their smaller counterparts. The equity gap in the UK is well publicised: the mainstream venture capital industry is rarely interested in making investments of less than £1m, and raising finance on the capital markets only becomes an option where more substantial sums are involved. Thus, only a few alternatives are available for small firms - often debt-related and with gearing and cash flow implications. Such options are generally costly.

EXIT ROUTES

One of the greatest concerns facing owner-managers is how they will exit from the business and realise their capital. Whether the ultimate aim is flotation, trade sale or succession, it is undoubtedly easier to promote a growing company. Investors are more likely to pay a premium for companies with critical mass or some kind of market dominance.

It is always a good discipline for the owner-manager to take a step back from his or her business in order to consider what a potential purchaser would find attractive about it. If the company is an inert local one and (as is all too often the case) is heavily dependent on a couple of key customers, it is unlikely to be attractive to prospective buyers. What the owner thought would be his or her pension fund may not, in fact, have any great value at all.

Whatever the chosen exit route, the key issue is how to groom the business for disposal. This may involve reviewing business strategy and removing personal assets and expenditure. The company's strategic plan should set out where the business is going and how its objectives are to be achieved. It should also ensure that, both for the owner and for the business itself, proper financial structures are in place that will allow these objectives to be met, i.e. the business must not be too highly geared and must be funded in the most appropriate way for its assets.

THE DOWNSIDES OF GROWTH

While growth companies are characterised by rapid increases in turnover, initially this may be accompanied by only a negligible rise in profitability and often an increased need for cash.

Therefore, in order to keep track of the company's financial position, the entrepreneur should establish a process for reporting and forecasting results and cash flows. He should also review the adequacy of the company's financial controls, which are often compromised with expansion, and set up new systems geared to meeting the business's future needs rather than its historic ones.

One reason for lower than anticipated profits is that growth companies are often sales-focused, taking on additional work or committing to additional orders without considering the impact on margins or, indeed, whether contracts are profitable at all. This may reflect a tendency to throw people at problems, based on the premise that because the company is growing, it can afford it.

The sales, rather than profit, focus is also likely to engender the symptom of a highly driven sales team who are rewarded on turnover rather than profits. It is therefore advisable for sales staff to be given guidance as to which products are profitable, and for the prices at which they are empowered to sell products to be very carefully set, with market conditions borne in mind. This may necessitate more complex commission structures, based partly on profits earned, and consequently a more sophisticated reporting and monitoring system.

In order for cash flow to be sustained, working capital needs careful management, since it usually increases at a rate exponential to the company's growth. For example, additional credit may be given to customers in order to generate further sales and stock levels may be increased to avoid running out of stock.

The owner-manager should regularly review the stock situation. Even by simply walking through the warehouse one can often see where there is overstocking – stockpiles of slow-moving lines are indicative of inadequate stock control. This vigilance should be supported by an effective stock system. If at all possible the computer system should facilitate a link between the perpetual inventory and purchase ordering procedures, as this will result in an efficient ordering process and reduce the likelihood of order duplication. The system can be further enhanced by incorporating sales ordering data.

THE NEXT ROUND

It is essential that the financial structures of a growing business are appropriate both to the company's and to the owner-manager's needs. Having overcome the financial and practical difficulties associated with initial growth, the challenge is then for the owner-manager to establish around him a management team that is capable of running the business efficiently and profitably.

With all these issues to address, the owner-manager may question whether he still wants to grow. Of course, some businesses will experience rapid growth relatively effortlessly, if there is a combination of drive from the top and a successful product or service offering, and some entrepreneurs relish the thrill of the deal or the challenge of developing their own product. However, all companies need continually to reinvent themselves by injecting new drive and ambition, otherwise they will be overtaken by their competitors, stagnate and eventually fail.

Chapter 2

The business plan

Andrew Garside, director of the Leeds office of 3i, Europe's leading venture capital company, highlights the crucial ingredients of an effective business plan

The facts of the matter are too well known to be denied – no business plan equals no business, eventually. Just existing is not a strategy. At the same time, the creation of a strong business plan, with all the teamwork and original thinking that entails, can have an extraordinarily uplifting effect on a firm.

As time goes on, the plan can become a living embodiment of your corporate vision and goal, serving as the benchmark against which your team, your investors and your lenders judge the company's performance. Who could argue against the value and efficacy of a business plan?

And yet the prospect of creating a business plan makes many people feel completely wretched. They seem to feel it has nothing to do with their real work but is something done wholly for the benefit of others – something which, finance-raising apart, is no more than a drain on the management team's time.

But the truth is otherwise. Good business plans are indeed the common factor linking all success stories. They are the route maps that take business people on a journey of value growth towards exit and personal reward.

THE "CRUNCH" ISSUES

And there is no mystery whatever about what makes them good. The basic elements that need to be covered are well enough known, and straightforward guidance can be found on many corporate finance-related websites (ours is at www.3i.com). But what are the crunch issues? Which factors decide whether your plan is good or not - in short, whether it is likely to attract finance?

At 3i we probably come across more business plans than most - we certainly fund hundreds of new transactions every year, and, as you can imagine, we see thousands of plans. The experience of reading and evaluating them and actually proceeding to work with successful companies has, over the years, given us some interesting insights into the common traits of good business plans. And this experience allows me to be both brutal and encouraging.

The brutal truth is that, sadly, many business plans are flawed in one or more of the key areas I am about to mention. The encouraging news is that many are not - and that there is no mystery involved, neither is the process of obtaining finance by any means a lottery.

It's my job to find opportunities for investment, whether that investment be £1m or £100m. We aren't looking for excuses to bin a proposal. On the contrary, we go out of our way to identify and support businesses that can show the magical ingredients: value growth opportunities and a good exit strategy. Magical? Certainly. Whether for the purposes of strategic guidance or finance-raising, a business plan's strength in these two areas is the most critical issue.

SIMPLICITY AND CLARITY ARE KEY

Before we proceed to review each of the crunch issues in turn, let's consider a couple of general points. First of all, every good business plan is both simple and crystal clear. For example, there's a firm in our portfolio whose business plan leaves you in no doubt whatsoever that a sale will be made to a trade buyer in three to four years' time. The strategy is immediately obvious.

More importantly, that strategy is applied and evident in every single item of the plan. It is not just left hanging on its own, as some airy nirvana to be hoped for. Each part of a business plan should have the strategic objective running right through it.

This is a critical indication of your ability to think clearly. A plan that shows your energies straying in several directions will indicate otherwise. Why, for example, if you are a skilled, quality manufacturer, should your business plan seek investment for some non-core activity, such as distribution? The implication is that you are unsure about the business you are in. Of course, it is sometimes right to develop new operations, but most businesses are very good at one particular thing.

KEEPING TO THE POINT

Whether the purpose of your business plan is to define and navigate your strategy or to attract finance, it needs to be clear. It also needs to be concise. I've seen five- to ten-page proposals that convince and 60-page ones that do not. The least helpful information is a flat and over-long description of a manufacturing process or business activity.

The most helpful is an explanation of why things are being done and the possible implications of doing them. A business plan should allow any informed reader to understand and evaluate the thinking and commercial position of the directors.

If your business plan shows that superior customer understanding has led you to negotiate a key new contract that will guarantee increased production and provide a substantial growth opportunity, then the case for new equipment to service that contract may well prove compelling.

But describing the new "Hokey Cokey 2000" from Germany in great detail and pointing out at length the expansion in production it will achieve does little to make the case. Those are general points, now let's move on to consider some of the sections that your business plan will include.

We shall start with the management section. Usually this is the space where you include the CVs of your senior team. That's fine, but you may be missing something as far as the external audience is concerned. Simply listing individual career histories does nothing to explain the dynamic between team members, and thus show how the whole may be greater than the sum of its parts.

It is, for example, very useful to hear the business leader explain why he included a certain person and what that person subsequently went on to add to the team effort. Expressed simply, in business language rather than gushing PR hype, this kind of information can add valuable colour to your plan – and give potential backers a far clearer picture of the team with which they are dealing. So, too, can the statement of your market position.

The depth of understanding of your own market that you demonstrate offers potential backers one of their best opportunities to evaluate your potential. What is being sought is specific evidence that you understand the needs of your customers – more than that, that you are modifying your product offering to suit the requirements of different customers. This isn't just a meaningless phrase: the businesses with the greatest growth potential really do seem to know their customers and their future requirements better than the customers themselves do.

EVALUATING MARKET TRENDS

Next comes your evaluation of market trends. Once more, the objective must be for you to put across a degree of insight and supporting rationale that shows the potential to deliver a strategic advantage. Occasionally a happy combination of time and place means that a business is onto a "dead cert". In most cases, however, the management is obliged to demonstrate an ability to stay ahead of the competition.

So what is the competition doing? More interestingly, what is it likely to do in the future and from where might fresh competition emerge? In the modern business environment, competitive pictures are far more complex and far more dynamic than the simple economic models might suggest. The next key competitor may be a totally new entrant to the market with an innovative approach.

If you set up as an Internet Service Provider just three years ago – were you predicting the entry of retail chains, banks, national newspapers and the like into your market, let alone competitors who offered the same service entirely free of charge?

Financial information is the next area to consider. The first rule is to be as thorough as possible. The second is that solid data means building from the bottom up rather than the top down. Calculating projected sales on the basis of what you expect from each individual customer will result in more credible figures than you would get if you simply made broad assumptions based on the headline numbers. If a business is not in a position to attempt decent, credible forecasts, it should recruit a good financial director fast, and certainly well before developing the business plan.

What about risks? The maxim here is to be open. We expect most management teams to be broadly optimistic – they wouldn't be doing the jobs they do otherwise. So, for the sake of balance, you need to show that risks are fully anticipated: If X were to happen, how would you react?

THE EXIT PLAN

Finally, and perhaps most importantly, we need to know what you are aiming for. Every business will eventually be sold or go bust – it's just a question of time. Your exit plan is, as mentioned earlier, one half of the magical element of the business plan. In the meantime, however, we need to see how you will make the business more valuable - the other half of the golden equation. We also need to think about who is likely to buy the business and why. If there is a certain type of trade buyer you have in mind, how could we make the business more attractive to them? How do your plans relate to the market cycle?

And will the market situation allow us to achieve a premium price? The level of profits you make is by no means a clear indication of the price you might get for the business. If, for example, the food retail market is polarising around corner stores and out-of-town superstores, the inherent profitability of your medium-sized town-centre chain may well make no difference in a market where this type of outlet is of no interest.

Thinking about the exit to this extent should not be confused with short-termism. Understanding value growth and exit potential is important in helping to build a business over the long term too.

So what will you do now? A good business plan is neither easy to create nor mysterious. But, regardless of finance, the basic question is this: how do you achieve value growth and a profitable exit without one?

Business plans do put the team under pressure, and under the spotlight. Weak areas emerge. The logic of past decisions and future plans is thoroughly tested. Figures must be made to add up. Every team member finds his or her thinking scrutinised and subject to debate. It's no longer enough just to run the business - and the load can seem unbearable.

Business plans undoubtedly create stress, but out of the stresses and tensions emerge blueprints for leadership. As they say at the gym: "No pain, no gain." Good business plans drive good businesses. They promote discipline and transparency. They offer a test-track to race new ideas on. They crystallise the attitudes, values and objectives that make your business different. They direct growth and express, with absolute clarity, the ultimate goal you are aiming for.

As a by-product of all these advantages - any of which would alone make the pain worthwhile – good business plans have a habit of attracting investment. There is no mystery, just plenty of hard work and even harder thinking. Whichever way you look at it, a good business plan is essential.

Chapter 3

Sources of finance

Henrietta Lake, small business correspondent on The Times, gives an overview of the various types of finance a company can access to fund growth

A business is like any other growing organism – forget to water and nourish it and it will quickly wither. At any stage in a company's development, the problem of the search for funds to sustain growth is not far away.

Unfortunately this does not mean that the hunt has become any easier. It requires painstaking research and constant review to ensure the most cost-effective, low-risk and convenient form of financing for the business at any point in time.

The easiest option, of course, is to rely on the owner's private funds or the company's retained profits – but often this does not produce enough capital to expand the enterprise to its full potential. Another port of call, also close to home, is capital borrowed from family and friends. After all, this source is likely to be reliable, usually involves preferential interest rates, and if anything went wrong the borrower would be more likely to be greeted with a flexible and understanding approach. But most company owners need to look a little further afield to find the pennies they need.

OVERDRAFTS

Borrowing from a bank in the form of a loan or overdraft remains the most popular form of external financing for most companies. Overdrafts are a simple and effective source of short-term finance. But, because they can be withdrawn by the bank at any time and have to be renegotiated every six to 12 months, they are best used to fund cash flow fluctuations and provide continuity financing.

Before the recession of the early 1990s companies tended to be too heavily reliant on overdrafts, so that when the banks pulled in their horns many firms were driven into liquidation. Since then businesses have been encouraged to switch to the more secure term loans. Overdrafts incur an arrangement fee, typically 2 per cent for a £5,000 facility. Interest is a fixed margin over base – usually between 1 and 5 per cent – although there is often room for negotiation on larger amounts.

TERM LOANS

Term loans should be used to provide fixed-term financing to cover development and start-up losses. They offer greater security than an overdraft because, unless the terms of the covenant are breached, the funds are assured for the full term. Traditionally, term loans have been secured with a personal guarantee or a fixed charge over property, fixed plant and machinery or debtors, with the bank lending up to between 50 and 70 per cent of the value of the property.

However over the past seven years there has been a marked tendency towards unsecured lending. Also, unlimited liability over third parties has now been abandoned. Costs include an arrangement fee, and often insurance such as critical illness cover. Fixed and variable interest rates can be arranged, as well as loans in different currencies in order to limit exchange-rate risks. For larger loans – typically £1m upwards – other, more complex arrangements can be provided, such as "swaps", which reduce costs through advanced financial engineering, or "caps", "floors" and "collars", which limit the interest paid on a floating-rate loan.

OTHER LOANS

Companies unable to secure a loan from a bank may be able to turn to the Small Firms Loan Guarantee (SFLG) which is expected to be subsumed by the new Enterprise Fund. This supports companies with high growth potential by providing a Government guarantee of up to 85 per cent against default for loans of between £5,000 and £250,000. Qualifying companies must have fewer than 200 employees and an annual turnover below £1.5m, or £3m for manufacturers. The Department for Education and Employment (DfEE) has a detailed list of eligible trades and sectors.

SFLGs cannot be used to replace existing loans or overdrafts. The borrower pays the lender as usual, plus a premium of 1.5 per cent per annum to the DTI on the outstanding amount of the loan. The premium is reduced to half a per cent if the loan is taken at a fixed rate of interest. The commercial aspects of the loan are a matter between the borrower and the lender.

Most larger cities have local loan schemes such as those run by local authorities or TECs, details of which are available at Business Links. Some finance houses are also now offering so-called "interest-free" loans, which are funded by making cost savings on a company's procurement, which is then balanced against the loan.

GRANTS

Grants can be time-consuming to apply for, but might be worth the effort if they postpone the need to borrow. There are many companies that offer advice on European and British grants for an upfront fee of around £300, but it is usually wiser to pay the fee once the grant has been awarded. Business Links give free advice on grants and have access to official grant directories. Information on grants can also be found at the economic development unit of the local county or borough council or at the Department of Trade and Industry's (DTI) regional offices, which have details of the many European Union grants that are available.

ASSET-BASED FINANCING

Asset finance can be used to raise greater sums than are available through traditional bank lending, since the packages allow you to spread the cost of acquiring an asset, which itself provides the main security. Payments are usually structured to match the life of the asset – particularly useful when you need to keep up with the latest equipment. Most such arrangements run for three to five years.

Packages fall into two main categories. The first is purchase arrangements, which encompass (a) the straightforward hire-purchase of items that are not expected to become obsolete in the near future, (b) lease purchase, involving lower monthly payments but a larger final payment, and (c) contract purchase, which includes servicing and maintenance and is often used for company vehicle fleets.

Second there are leases, which allow you to use the asset for the term of the lease without ever acquiring it outright. At the end of the most straightforward finance lease, the asset is sold to a third party and the borrower receives the proceeds as an agreed rebate. Lower payments can be made for an operating lease, but in this case there are no proceeds from the ultimate sale; another option is contract hire, which includes servicing and maintenance. Costs are similar to those of an overdraft, but an accountant should be consulted over the various tax implications of asset-based financing.

FACTORING

Factoring originated in the US in the 1960s to address the problem of late-paying customers and a shortage of working capital. It is a flexible procedure that allows companies to raise finance on the basis of the value of outstanding invoices. Usually within around 24 hours of invoicing a customer, the factor pays the company a proportion of the invoice amount, typically 70-80 per cent, and then collects the debt on its behalf. The balance, less charges, is paid on collection. However, the company remains responsible for reimbursing the factor for bad debts, unless a "non-recourse facility" has been purchased.

Factoring is not suitable for firms with complex contracts involving stage payments or interim claims, or for those with a very small customer base. Full audits of the company will be carried out by the factor to assess profitability and a £200,000 turnover is usually the minimum. Set credit limits will be imposed on each of the firm's customers. Factoring charges comprise interest and administration fees – the latter being based on turnover, the volume of invoices and the number of customers. Export factoring is another useful facility, minimising the risk of conducting business overseas. (This issue is covered extensively in Chapter 5.)

INVOICE DISCOUNTING

Invoice discounting is a tool for larger businesses with well-established credit management procedures that require faster access to the money tied up in debtor balances. It works in a similar way to factoring except that the company maintains control of the sales ledger and collects its own debts – the discounter simply provides the finance. This gives the company more control over and confidentiality with its clients. Once it receives a copy of an invoice, the invoice discounter makes available a proportion of the amount concerned. When the firm receives payment from its customer it must deposit the money with the discounter, which then pays the remainder of the invoice amount minus fees.

But the requirements for this form of finance are stricter than those for factoring: annual turnover has to be above £500,000 and audits will be carried out every three months to make sure credit control is in order. A mixture of factoring and invoice discounting can be arranged. The Factors and Discounters Association (FDA) can supply a list of factors, itemising the services they provide and stating their turnover requirements.

EQUITY FINANCE

Raising capital through equity finance, whether it be a stock market flotation or venture capital, is an effective way to bolster a balance sheet and can make other lenders, such as banks, more willing to lend on the back of it. (This issue is covered in depth in Chapter 7.)

VENTURE CAPITAL

The need for venture capital has become more acute as other sources of finance, such as banks, wary of the risk of supplying large sums of money to growing firms, and stockmarket flotations became less attractive as a result of the low valuations and poor liquidity of smaller stocks.

A venture capitalist supplies unsecured financing, usually of sums in excess of £250,000, in return for a proportion of the company's shares. A projected return of 25 per cent within three to five years is the least a venture capitalist will settle for, and targets as high as 30-40 per cent are common. The argument is that this is justified by the risk venture capitalists take in backing growth companies. With almost one in four deals failing, extra pressure is put on the remaining companies to make up the shortfall.

Venture capitalists look for a team with a good management track record, products and services with a strong competitive edge, owners willing to sell their shares, realistic and detailed business plans, and a clear exit plan within a defined timescale, in the form of a trade sale or repurchase. Competition for deals is tough – for every plan the venture capitalists accept, tens more are rejected. (See Chapter 2 for a fuller account of the venture capitalists' objectives.)

BUSINESS ANGELS

These are wealthy individuals willing to provide a company with capital in exchange for a proportion of its shares. But these deals are more personal and comparatively informal in comparison with venture capital. They will fund sums well below £250,000 as well as providing early-stage capital. The expected returns may be slightly lower than those of the venture capitalists because angels are often looking for rewards beyond the purely financial.

Business angels are particularly useful in that they bring their own experience, skills and often contacts to the table. This characteristic makes individual chemistry with the company directors important, since angels will usually demand close involvement in the firm, such as a seat on the board. Angels offer more flexibility than venture capitalists, and the initial negotiations need not be as protracted. But, as with venture capital, competition for funding is tough. Business angels can be found either informally or by approaching an "introduction" service such as the National Business Angels Network, which matches potential investors with businesses seeking finance.

FRANCHISING

Franchising is an ideal way for an established business to raise capital and expand quickly by selling its trademark. The firm wishing to expand enters into an agreement with a franchisee, who buys the right to operate using the franchisor's trademark and sometimes its stock and equipment. The franchisee pays an initial fee of anything between £5,000 and £500,000, plus ongoing fees from its profits.

However, franchising is suitable only for particular business cultures, products and services. Franchisees are business partners, not employees, and must be managed accordingly. Businesses that can be run as branch networks suit franchising best. The formula must be easily replicated, and premises should be easy to find and capable of being fitted out quickly. The process also has to be easy to learn, as it must be possible to teach someone else how to operate the business even if they have no experience in the field. And franchises only work if they are profitable on both sides, so low-margin businesses need not apply.

There are numerous grants available to support franchising. However, it is accepted wisdom that if a firm does not have sufficient funds to finance the project itself, it should not be franchising in the first place. Consultants', lawyers' and accountants' fees, plus the cost of marketing to potential franchisees, add up on average to around £6,000 per franchise.

Chapter 4

Controlling growth: the role of the non-financial director

Weak financial management is a key cause of business failure. But, stresses Bob Earnshaw, managing director of Management Development and Training, this issue affects not only the finance director, but all board directors

You could argue that there is no such thing as a non-financial director. Of course we are not all tax experts, legal experts or financial systems experts. That is why we have highly qualified members of the board who carry the title financial director.

ACROSS THE BOARD

However, the board as a whole is collectively responsible for the protection of the assets of the organisation, the protection of the creditors and shareholders and generally keeping the business in business. The financial director cannot carry this responsibility alone. Like it or not, every operating decision that is made on behalf of the company will have a financial implication somewhere along the line. Growth may involve new products, new markets and new and unfamiliar customers. How liquid are they? Are different credit terms involved in securing rapid market penetration?

It should be the role of every member of the board to partic-ipate in getting the right balance between market risk and financial risk. When focusing on financing the growth of the organisation, the first step is to secure and maintain a strong financial platform as a base for that growth and everyone is involved. It all boils down to good financial housekeeping.

HOUSEKEEPING

Good financial housekeeping presupposes a meaningful financial dialogue at board level. For many non-financial directors a major barrier to constructing that dialogue is understanding financial language and concepts. Every director should make a determined effort to get over that barrier. It is no longer sufficient to rely on the financial director to act as an interpreter, since every customers', suppliers' and competitors' financial statements, which should be monitored regularly, are written in the same language.

MANAGING THE PROFIT AND LOSS ACCOUNT

It is important to remember that the Profit & Loss Account (P&L) is a performance document and not a cash-in, cash-out document and includes both cash and credit transactions for a given period.

It often comes as a surprise to many non-financial directors to discover that P&L numbers are not as cut-and-dried as they had imagined. The complexity of today's organisations requires the financial director and his or her team to make frequent judgements and assumptions about sales, costs, expenses and profits for the period. Of course there are rules and regulations, but complexity throws up grey areas concerning asset values and the timing of financial events.

If non-financial directors are to use financial information as part of their decision-making process they need to know of what judgements and assumptions those numbers are based on and, sometimes, go as far as challenging some of those judgements. It will always be difficult to get an answer to the question, "Is it right or is it wrong?" It makes much more sense to ask, "Is it useful?" Do the numbers really reflect the way the business operates? This is particularly pertinent to managerial financial statements, as opposed to the statutory reporting of an organisation.

The difference between how financial information is organised internally and the how it is reported to the outside world is essentially a level of detail and, in many cases, frequency. Certainly, the level of detail contained in published reports would be inadequate when it comes to monitoring the profit performance of different parts of the business. It may be useful, for example, to separate the costs of the business into fixed and variable portions, an analysis that certainly cannot be found on a published P&L. A variable cost is a cost that remains the same per unit of activity but varies directly with volume. A fixed cost does not vary directly with volume.

By taking the sales less the variable cost one gets a profit number usually known as "contribution". This is the contribution to covering the fixed costs of the business and profit. This sort of analysis gives a different view of where profit is really generated. In many cases different operating areas, different products or different services, deliver different contributions. While accepting that there are marketplace constraints, is it possible to manage product lines or reallocate marketing resources to maximise contribution? Do financial systems provide enough transparency to enable one to use this sort of analysis?

Non-financial directors are the prime users of internal financial information and should be active in determining the level of detail and the frequency of that information. In periods of rapid growth, they may require more information or need to change the frequency of financial reporting. However, there is the danger that everything can be over-engineered. So, think about adding value and apply the "useful" test.

MANAGING THE BALANCE SHEET

It is not managing the Profit & Loss account, however, that keeps companies in business. Why is it that many of the companies that are forced into liquidation are making a profit? The main reason is that they simply run out of cash. This is often because they failed to manage the balance sheet.

This problem is particularly acute during periods of rapid growth. Anyone can plan to be profitable but a company about to embark on a significant growth should ask itself whether it has the resources necessary to support that step forward. In the words of one former managing director, "We sold so much we went broke doing it!" It is probably fair to say that most directors are relatively familiar with some form of the Profit & Loss Account but the Balance Sheet often remains a mystery and is traditionally the domain of the finance director. But who is responsible for collecting from debtors? There are a number of players involved in the process of managing the balance sheet:

■ *Who made the sale in the first place?*

■ *Who is responsible for managing stock levels?*

■ *Who is responsible for signing off large amounts of money for capital investments in fixed assets and the profit they will generate subsequently?*

■ *Who should be concerned about adequate levels of financing, whether it be debt or equity and the effect on the cost of capital and the liquidity of the company?*

Clearly, the responsibility does not lie solely with the finance director. Contributing to the management of assets is one of the most important roles of all directors, financial or not.

PLANNING

Too often the problems begin at the planning stage and especially when planning for growth. Traditionally the planning focus of most small and medium-sized companies has been sales, volumes, costs and profits or, in other words, P&L. How often do companies set planning objectives for managing assets?

The ability to re-jig the fixed assets over a short period of time is naturally somewhat limited. This is a long-term investment strategy. However, a company can significantly influence its investment in working capital during the operating cycle of the business. For example, has the sales and marketing director set targets for Debtor Days? Having made the sale do the directors get regular reports on this asset and do they know about the ageing of debtors, those going out 60, 70, 80 days? This may well be where the exposure is. Again, how close can the production director get to the "just-in-time" principle in managing stock levels? Can we get the optimal balance between pushing less volume through the fixed cost of production and, therefore, the effect of that on cost and profit, and the liquidity effect of carrying high stocks?

When it comes to long-term assets, is the company taking advantage of discounted cash-flow techniques – and the profitability measures that are derived from them – to make decisions on capital investments where the payback period is long enough to justify this approach?

And what about acquisitions? Who decides on the goodwill number? It is the role of all directors to ask these questions, get the answers and, in the interest of improved balance sheet management, implement action plans based on the answers.

Failure to assume this role may incur hidden cost to the business. As an example, if a company allows customers to take excessive amounts of credit, it is tying cash up in financing debtors, preventing it from being available to make profitable short-term investments or reduce debt financing and save interest. This loss of opportunity is the opportunity cost to the company of free financing someone else's company!

CASH FLOW MANAGEMENT

Cash is king. It is always worth remembering that happiness is a positive cash flow!

The issue of cash flow management is addressed thoroughly in Chapter 5. It is worth saying here, however, that the main objective of managing the P&L and Balance Sheet more effectively is to secure adequate cash flowing through the business to finance growth and to take full advantage of market opportunities. Of course, providing a company's financial performance will allow, it can always re-finance itself through additional debt or equity. However, the cheapest source of cash is the self-generated cash flow from operations. Who is responsible for operations? The non-financial director.

Chapter 5

Managing your cash flow and credit

Patricia M Scott FCCA FCT, chief executive of The Chieveley Group, warns of the problems resulting from poor cash flow management and stresses the benefits gained from getting it right

A time of growth is an exciting period for everyone in a company, board and employees alike. It is also a demanding time, requiring ample reserves of confidence, commitment, energy and vision. The last thing anyone needs at a time like this is to run out of money.

Yet it's at just such a time that the directors need to be aware of this very real possibility, for growth is very demanding of cash. Overstretching – running out of cash and available borrowing lines – is a real risk that needs to be understood, assessed and managed. Growth consumes cash in two ways:

■ *In funding capital expenditure needed as the company invests in increased capacity; and*

■ *In funding higher working capital as the company "gears up" to meet increasing sales demands.*

Either of these factors, if allowed to spiral out of control, could bring the growth to an abrupt end, or at least involve top management in messy and time-consuming liquidity negotiations.

The most difficult credit crisis to manage is the unexpected one. To lenders, a cash crisis is a sign that management are not controlling the business efficiently. Anticipated cash needs will always receive a more sympathetic hearing than crisis needs.

Capital expenditure appears to be straightforward. The project can be costed, finance raised, capacity increased. The danger lies in two areas: the possibility that the project will overrun (a) its cost budget, or (b) its time budget, which would mean the company having to source increased capacity from elsewhere at a higher cost than planned.

Working capital is subtler, and can creep up on management when their attention is fixed elsewhere – on generating business and meeting demanding delivery schedules. Working capital escalates as a result of:

■ *Increasing stocks to enable the company to meet new levels of demand. This is exacerbated if slow-moving items are not managed;*

■ *Increasing debtors. If customers pay one month in arrears, the inputs needed to create supplies have to be funded for that period. As turnover increases, so does the cash needed to fund the inputs. New customers with unproven payment records may exacerbate the problem, as will bad debts;*

■ *As the company increases orders on suppliers to meet higher levels of demand, they may demand payment more swiftly until the company has built up a reliable track record.*

These trends, unmanaged, can lead to inconvenience and, in extreme cases, disaster.

So how does a hard-pressed board ensure that growth can be financed, in terms of both availability of funds and cost? The answer lies in the anticipation of needs and management against budget. This requires investment in people, systems and time. At a time when resources are already overstretched, and the cost base is growing, many companies resist this type of investment. Employing more people to manage funding and working capital can be regarded as a non-productive overhead.

Time spent on forecasting, which diverts attention away from growing the business, may be regarded as a bureaucratic nuisance adding little value. I hope this chapter will demonstrate the possible adverse consequences sufficiently to convince directors of the value to be added by good project and working-capital management.

FACTORING COMES OF AGE

Recent research among accountants suggests that factoring and invoice discounting are overcoming their traditional image as the "last chance saloon" for shaky businesses. As far as accountants are concerned, at least, factoring is now widely recognised as an important financial tool for growing companies.

The survey, carried out by trade publication Accountancy Age in conjunction with the Bibby Group of Factors, attracted more than 200 replies from accountants, with around three-quarters in practice and the rest in commerce.They were asked to rank five different types of business finance on the basis of cost-effectiveness. The bank overdraft and bank term loan were the accountants' preferred forms of business finance, each attracting just under 22 per cent of first place ratings. But factoring and invoice discounting came only marginally behind, with more than 21 per cent rating it as their preferred financing method. Private investors and venture capital were favoured by 18 per cent.

A previous survey on the same subject carried out four years ago found private investors to be the most cost-effective finance source with the bank overdraft close behind, followed by venture capital. Factoring and invoice discounting were in fourth place, with the bank term loan last.

The survey also suggests that well over a third of accountants would recommend factoring for a company's growth or expansion. A further one-in-four see it as most appropriate for credit control. Only 20 per cent of respondents saw factoring as best suited to recovery/turnaround.

Just over half of all the survey's respondents, however, admitted that either they or their clients had reservations about factoring as a source of business finance. Of these, 34 per cent cited cost as the problem, while 29 per cent cited the business community's perception of factoring. A typical quote in answer to the question: "What reservations do you have about factoring?" was: "None, but clients continue to have reservations over cost and status".

Accountants' basic knowledge of factoring and invoice discounting has increased in recent years. The latest survey shows 46 per cent claiming "considerable knowledge", 53 per cent "some" and just one per cent "little or none". This compares with 17 per cent, 61 per cent and a surprising 22 per cent, respectively, in 1995.

FORECASTING THE NEED

Forecasting must cover enough time to allow the board to judge the adequacy of borrowing lines. If the use of any individual source of funds is restricted, this needs to be taken into account. If the forecast indicates that insufficient lines are available, now is the time to make arrangements for additional sources, if possible.

What is a sufficient period for forecasting? The board needs to make a judgement, but six or 12 months may be appropriate, rather than over the entire period of the business plan. Some may argue that, in a time of growth, the future is too unpredictable to allow for forecasting. The answer to this is not to forego forecasting altogether, but to forecast prudently. It is better to find that you have too many lending lines than too few.

One more word of caution. A time of growth is a time of optimism, but optimistic forecasting of cash is counterproductive. Guard against overoptimism and try to forecast realistically. Is the rate of sales increase realistic or optimistic? Are customers really paying as quickly as forecast? Just half a dozen simple "sense tests" will ensure that the numbers are good for use.

Revisit the forecast regularly. If actual performance starts to slide away, particularly if the business is using more cash than was forecast, an urgent re-evaluation will be necessary. The time to do this is now - not when the bank starts bouncing cheques.

MINIMISING THE NEED

The other side of cash flow management is ensuring that the cash demands of the business are minimised, without standing in the way of value-enhancing growth. On the large capital project, cash demands are minimised:

■   *At the design stage, by rigorously demanding that each element of cost is justified. He who has the lowest cost base has competitive advantage. If the same outputs can be achieved with a lower specification of building or machine – without disadvantage in the long term – then good management demands the lower-cost option.*

■ *During the construction/production stage, by having a project manager keep close track of progress, including costs. Any costs in excess of those budgeted must be subject to a rigorous clearing process. It is not the job of your supplier to determine whether or not the additional charges are acceptable to you.*

Working capital management is more complex. The complexity should not put you off, however, for it is the creeping escalation of working capital that can bring about a sudden and unexpected crisis in financing. Working capital management will focus on three main areas: stocks, debtors and creditors.

1) Stocks

As turnover grows, so stock is also likely to grow. The requirement for stock minimisation and the need to be in a position to meet all orders swiftly set up two contrary tensions. Some companies have turned to techniques such as "just-in-time processing" to help minimise stocks. Some hints for stock minimisation are:

■ *Negotiate the tightest possible delivery terms from suppliers;*

■ *If manufacturing, eliminate all avoidable delays as the product moves through process systems;*

■ *Track sales by product, ensuring that orders for fast-moving stock are made regularly rather than occasionally in bulk;*

■ *Examine slow-moving stock to determine whether the ranges are still economic.*

2) Debtors

Debtors are people who owe you money, your customers to whom you have sold goods on credit. In cash terms, a sale has not taken place until the customer pays you. Your company is at risk on debtors in two ways:

■ *The risk of late payers. In these cases, you will have to continue to finance the debtor until receipt of cash. Too many of these can impact seriously on working capital, and the overall level of finance required by the business;*

■ *The risk of bad debts – instances in which you will never receive the cash. A significant bad-debt level can easily cripple a growing company.*

Tight credit control is essential for the growing business. In the enthusiasm for increased turnover, it is easy to lose sight of this vital reality. Tips for credit control are:

■ *Make credit checks and follow up references, particularly where significant levels of credit are being considered. Don't be afraid of putting customers off. A good customer will respect you for checking his credit;*

■ *Allocate credit limits that escalate as a customer's payment record becomes proven. Continue to make periodic checks. Any company's financial position can change;*

■ *Nominate a responsible individual to take charge of your debtor management. Unpaid accounts should be identified imme-diately they become overdue;*

■ *Develop policies for dealing with overdue accounts, starting with a reminder and moving to legal action where necessary. Ensure that the actions are implemented. Keep the money flowing into your business;*

■ *Make sure that you look long and hard at whether overdue customers continue to be supplied with additional goods. The more goods you supply to an overdue customer, the larger the risk you take. You will have to use judgement, but be tough when necessary. Sympathy for somebody else's problems could drag your business down too.*

3) Creditors

These are the people to whom you owe money: suppliers of goods and services. Money paid out to suppliers has to be financed by your business, so the target is to ensure that you pay these people as late as is commercially feasible. This is not to imply that you act irresponsibly: open dialogue with suppliers is far more productive.

The following practices can will help to achieve your objectives:

- *At the start of a relationship, negotiate the best terms you can possibly get. The longer you are given to pay, the less pressure on your growing business's finances;*

- *Look into the ways you pay your bills. Cheques can give you several days' grace as compared to electronic transfer, but can cost more in charges and administration time;*

- *Develop policies on payment timing, and keep to them. Your long-term business relationships are important, so unnecessary delay in making payments is inadvisable.*

MEETING THE NEED

Having determined how much cash you need, and ensured by good project and working capital management that the amount is as low as possible, where do you get the cash?

The world of finance offers a variety of financing possibilities. Unfortunately, for the smaller company, it is probable that the options will be limited to the more traditional finance sources:

1. *Capital from owners, venture capital providers and business angels;*

2. *Finance from banks;*

3. *Reducing working capital via invoice discounting and factoring.*

The first is a topic all of its own, and is included here purely in the interests of completeness. (For more information, see Chapter 3.)

Apart from capital, most small and medium-sized businesses will source the bulk of their finance from the banks. For a small business this will usually be only one or, at the most, two banks.

Long-term projects, where the cash will be needed for an extended time, should ideally be financed by a long-term loan, probably secured on the plant or facility to be financed. A long-term loan may cost more, but gives a certain peace of mind about one chunk of the finance, for the life of the loan at least.

CASE STUDY

FACTORING THE MODERN WAY

Brighton-based Computer and Network Consultants provides IT solutions and technical support to a wide range of clients, from SMEs to blue chip organisations such as Fuller, Smith & Turner, Hoverspeed and Acxiom. Since its formation in February 1996, it has used factoring as a means of financing business growth.

Director Gary Jowett says he and his fellow directors had encountered factoring before and immediately recognised that it would be suitable for them when they started the business. They approached Maddox Bibby Factors – part of the UK's largest independent factoring group – because they wanted a factor that was not affiliated to a high street bank. They did not want to have to conform to what they feared would be the inflexible rules and constraints of a large institution.

Computer and Network Consultants uses factoring in what Jowett describes as "the modern way" – as a convenient way of collecting payment, rather than as a financial lifeline as some businesses do. He reckons the company would probably have to employ two people to handle the sales ledger, but by factoring it can collect cash far more cost-effectively.

In addition, because it factors, it does not have the problem of having to approach the bank to ask for an overdraft every time it wins a big contract. The flexibility the business derives from factoring gives Jowett and his colleagues the confidence to know they can handle anything that comes their way, without worrying how to finance it.

Factoring has helped Computer and Network Consultants to establish both an impressive client base and a sound financial future. The company has taken on three more staff and is growing steadily, with its first year turnover of £1m expected to hit the £2m mark this year.

Working capital will be financed in the first instance by bank overdraft. Bank overdrafts work well provided the company does not present the bank with too many surprises. Surprises lead to credit concerns, which in turn can lead to unexpected demands for repayment. Therefore:

■ *Try to negotiate a limit in excess of your peak forecast needs, to give yourself headroom for slippages;*

■ *Keep on top of working capital (see above), constantly reforecasting, particularly for the short term, so that you see where borrowings are headed;*

■ *If you foresee a need higher than your overdraft limit, talk to the bank as early as possible. You are far more likely to get a sympathetic hearing (and more finance) if you anticipate problems and share them, together with your proposed solutions.*

Many growing companies also find that factoring or discounting their invoices takes pressure off working capital and overdraft requirements, and can be an extremely helpful additional source of finance. These facilities often also offer credit insurance at a price. This removes concerns about bad debts, although the factor will usually impose his own credit exposure limits per customer. Factoring is dealt with in more detail elsewhere in this guide.

CONCLUSION

In conclusion, what are the tools for successfully financing growth?

■ *First, be aware of likely cash requirements by forecasting both capital projects and working capital;*

■ *Second, invest in people, systems and time to manage capital projects and working capital. Keep stocks as low as possible, look at just-in-time processing and minimisation of delivery delays with suppliers. Keep debtors under control by credit checking and prompt, decisive action over late payers. Negotiate as much time as possible to pay suppliers.*

■ *Third, maintain good relationships with your providers of finance. Ensure that you have their confidence, and you are more likely to have their support when you need it. In other words, treat financing of the company's growth as an important part of the growth itself, and your business can only benefit in the long term.*

ASSET-BASED FINANCE

David Marsden, chairman of the Factors and Discounters Association describes the merits of factoring and invoice discounting for growing companies

The key to managing business growth is to monitor and maximise cash flow. Previously, funding methods for businesses have been rigid, based solely on historical performance and value of business assets, ignoring future potential. The rapid development of the factoring and invoice discounting industry has successfully redressed this by offering a more flexible and growing source of finance than the traditional bank overdraft or loan.

Now used by over 24,000 companies, asset-based finance has continued to progress since the economic recovery of the early nineties. Advances to our clients have more than trebled from £1.3bn in 1992 to £4.4bn in 1998. Last year our members handled over £56bn of sales for our clients.

One of the main reasons for the continued growth of factoring and invoice discounting is the significant benefits offered to businesses compared with the relatively inflexible arrangements of a bank overdraft. A bank manager will often set a limit which may not keep pace with a business's requirements for working capital, especially if the business is expanding; the reduction of a facility at short or no notice does not provide a solid foundation for long-term financial planning.

The most tangible benefit of factoring and invoice discounting is a dramatic improvement in cash flow, which in turn enables a company to fund its growth and plan its investment. In the case of factoring, the factor takes care of the credit control. This gives the management more time to spend on marketing and business strategy and can improve relationships with customers by helping to ensure a clear and consistent approach to debt collection.

Factoring can help ensure the company's level of working capital complements the rise in its sales, giving it the momentum and confidence it needs to continue to move forward, as well as allowing a business to negotiate better discounts with suppliers for prompt payment or bulk purchases to support its sales.

Over the next few years, more growth is expected for the asset based finance industry, as businesses and their financial advisers come to understand its benefits better. The industry continues to develop, particularly in the use of information technology, such as the Internet. This means that its services will continue to improve and it will become the finance method of choice for more and more SMEs.

Chapter 6

Are banks doing the business?

Banks provide a substantial proportion of external small company finance. Mark Anstead, business writer, assesses whether the banks are meeting small businesses' needs

The Institute of Directors, the British Chambers of Commerce and the Federation of Small Businesses have all reported their members running into problems raising loans from banks. The issue was strong enough to prompt a Government review into whether there is enough competition in the banking industry.

Central to the review was that the concern that small firms may be at the mercy of a banking oligopoly that sets inappropriately high interest rates on loans. The review included a comparison between the UK and US, where there are over 600 different banks to choose from and a more competitive market.

While Don Cruickshank, the former telecoms regulator heading the review, quickly widened its scope to look at consumer banking services as well, concerns about small businesses remained at the heart of the brief. High technology firms in particular, as noted by the Bank of England's report into *The Financing of Small Firms*, appeared typically to be lacking in plant and machinery to use as collateral, often facing rejection as a result.

The Government has historically sought to ease the collateral problem through its Small Firms' Loan Guarantee Scheme. But this scheme is not adequately promoted by the banks, who begrudge bearing the brunt of the administration costs involved.

Has the general over-insistence on security forced small businesses to rely on overdrafts? If so, it is a dangerous practice given that this was the principal reason why so many businesses failed in the recession of the early nineties. As the economy slowed, banks began to recall overdrafts and those businesses that had overstretched themselves did not survive the process.

But it is difficult to establish the real truth in all these accusations ahead of Cruickshank's findings. The Bank of England stoutly maintains that small businesses are enjoying a better relationship with their banks than ever before, and that many are avoiding reliance on overdrafts, more readily considering alternative forms of finance (including factoring and invoice discounting).

In order to establish the truth, the review team asked banks to describe how they decide whether or not to grant applications for loans, and to state the extent of local discretion allowed. They also wanted to know what incentives operate for decision-makers, and how credit worthiness is scored and interest rates set.

Cruickshank published his interim report in July 1999. In it he was fiercely critical of the banks' general unwillingness to co-operate and disclose information. However, little mention was made of the issues the review was supposed to be investigating, and Cruickshank has argued that unless the banks become more co-operative he will not be able to file a report until 2000.

Regardless of how the debate turns out, it has served to highlight a number of key ways in which small businesses can strengthen their chances of good service from a bank:

1 *Communicate well and stay in touch;*

2 *Carefully acquire market intelligence for your business plan;*

3 *Promote your business advisers;*

4 *Consider the most suitable form of loan funding to apply for;*

5 *Recruit experienced non-executive directors.*

COMMUNICATION

According to research by the Forum of Private Business, a small-business lobby group, a small business with a poor banking relationship is four times more likely to have a loan application rejected than one that enjoys a relationship of mutual trust and co-operation.

Too many businesses don't make an effort to build their bank relationship until the last minute, at which point it feels one-sided. The more your bank manager knows about the details of your business ahead of any application, the better. If your bank is already familiar with you and your market it can only serve to help your case or facilitate a faster decision.

YOUR BUSINESS PLAN

Bankers feel out of their depth with high technology firms. They do not understand the market, let alone the product, and they justifiably feel that the sector has a tendency to forecast high growth rates backed by insubstantial evidence of potential sales.

But it isn't only high technology firms that fall into the trap of formulating unintelligible business plans. The onus is on the small business to make a loan application easy to assess, which means spending more time and attention on your marketing argument. Consider getting external marketing advice at this stage – someone who can scour through the plan converting it to plain English and adding general marketing wisdom.

Overall it is the market case that appeals to lenders and investors. Be realistic and make sure you can substantiate your assumptions. Deliberately overestimate costs and think carefully about the financial implications of success. For example, if you are seeking finance for new machinery, have you adequately estimated your financial needs when it comes to additional stock required? (See Chapter 2 for a full account of writing the right business plan.)

BUSINESS ADVISERS

There is a common evolutionary pattern to the start-up of a small business. It usually begins with funding from personal savings and input from family or friends. There may be a private investor involved and at some stage the bank will be approached.

As the business begins to grow, so it acquires professional advisers, as and when needed. First an accountant, then legal input. Recruitment and marketing consultants are often not approached until a much later stage.

The trouble with this model is that it is by far the least attractive proposition to a bank. Established and historic relationships with key business partners offering legal, financial, marketing and recruitment advice constitute an asset that may lever greater co-operation from financial institutions.

Put bluntly, the bank can see who it is they are going to have to trust. List these relationships at the head of your business plan, together with your partners' own client lists. This reassures the bank that they are not the only source of external advice, and that the risk is thus less severe. It is far better to establish these relationships before you need them, at minimal annual cost for basic advice, than to bear the brunt of a financial problem when you are unable to raise the finance you need.

APPROPRIATE FORMS OF LOAN FUNDING

The overdraft is the simplest form of borrowing, but should be used mainly for short-term cash flow needs, not to finance capital investments. For this latter purpose, a commonplace and more suitable financial tool you might choose is a standard floating-rate loan, particularly if you anticipate that interest rates will be coming down in the near future or if you foresee a healthy future cash flow enabling early repayment.

Otherwise the bank manager will probably want to steer you towards a fixed-rate, fixed-term product. If your business is sensitive to changes in interest rates, or if you need fine control over costs, then this is clearly the best option and gives your bank the chance to peg the repayment term to the useful lifetime of the asset you wish to acquire.

A variety of more sophisticated products are on offer for larger amounts, and every bank will have its own range of options and details about these. Such products tend to involve making either financial or non-financial covenants (eg. promising that the loan will never exceed a percentage of net worth, or agreeing to produce quarterly management figures). But with these loans you may be able to negotiate more flexible terms, such as repayment holidays to cover seasonal cash flow problems.

NON-EXECUTIVE DIRECTORS

There is anecdotal evidence to suggest that careful recruitment of non-executive directors with a background in your industry can have a beneficial influence on your success with a bank. This principle certainly operates when attempting to raise venture capital, so much so that the money often comes with a few non-executives attached to it.

The argument is similar to the point made above about listing your key business partners, but this time it is the structure of your own management team that is in the spotlight. An owner-manager certainly can't function as a jack-of-all-trades, so he or she needs to prove that the company is able to draw upon a useful pool of experience through its personnel.

It may be worth considering scouting around for successful entrepreneurs who, having already achieved success for their own companies, are willing and available to pass on their advice and become involved. The commitment needn't be high, mostly involving attendance at strategic board meetings throughout the year, and you might consider offering a small equity holding in return for their time.

Whatever arrangements you have made in respect of non-executives, the lesson here appears to be: don't choose only people with whom you naturally "gel", but keep in mind the criterion of trying to impress a bank manager with the track record of your extended team.

BANKS' SUPPORT FOR GROWING BUSINESSES

'What can my bank do for me?' is a question many owners of growing businesses probably ask of themselves, but how many ask it of their bank? Banks have moved a long way from the simple days of current account, overdraft and money transmission and now offer a vast range of services, suitable for businesses at different stages of growth, says Andy Brenan, Director, British Bankers' Association

The bank manager can provide access to these services and by asking the right questions can tailor services to the needs of a business at a particular point in time, but the person with the most knowledge about

BANKS' SUPPORT FOR GROWING BUSINESSES

the future direction of a business is the business owner. It therefore makes sense for the business owner to keep the bank manager up-to-date with future plans, so that they can work on these plans together.

Most banks produce sophisticated guides and planning tools to help businesses start up and expand by understanding their own needs. Many of these are available on disk or CD-Rom and use of these will demonstrate to the bank manager that a business owner has thought about the road ahead in a structured way.

Banks recognise the different needs of businesses by employing specialists in areas such as technology-based industries, professional practices, electronic banking, trade-finance and franchising, to name just a few. The essential thing is that no matter how specialised the plans of a business, the same question should still be asked of the bank: "What can my bank do for me?"

The choice of finance options for growing businesses is greater than ever. The days of the overdraft as the principal form of business funding are long gone, with term finance the norm and fixed rate funding adding a degree of certainty to future repayments for an increasing number of businesses. Where conventional finance is not appropriate, banks can offer factoring and discounting, asset finance and some are experimenting with venture capital alongside their more traditional offerings. When a business will benefit from grants or soft loan schemes, banks are able to signpost local initiatives which may be of assistance.

In addition to their mainstream lending activities, many banks are involved in local micro-credit schemes, usually in partnership with Councils, Enterprise Agencies or Business Links. These schemes often provide a higher level of advice and training for business owners and aim to promote regeneration of an area through encouraging entrepreneurship. The BBA has produced an inventory of such schemes which will shortly be available on our web site: www.bba.org.uk

It is difficult to do justice in such a short space to the vast array of bank services available to growing businesses. For this reason the key message must be for the business owner to ask regularly of their bank: 'What can you do for me?'

Chapter 7

Raising equity capital

New equity offers companies a more substantial financial foundation then can ever be achieved by relying solely on debt. David Brooks, senior corporate finance partner at Grant Thornton, reports

There comes a time in business when the directors are faced with the possibility of taking a giant step forward – going boldly into areas they have never been before. However, to do so will require capital, which in the majority of cases will mean having to give up a slice of "your" business to a third party.

Parting with some of the shareholding value that you have spent years creating or taking on an investment partner for a new business start-up can be a formidable task. However securing new equity finance may provide just the bridge you need to take you and your business onto a different plain.

BUSINESS ANGELS

Where relatively low levels of equity are required, wealthy individuals or "Business Angels" are probably the best route.

It is estimated that there are currently some 18,000 Business Angels in the UK, who invest around £350m a year into about 3,500 business. Generally speaking they fall into one of three categories: patron, entrepreneurial and occupational.

The patron angel typically has £1m to invest and will require little involvement in the day-to-day running of the business. The entrepreneurial angel has between £50,000 and £1m to invest and will probably be looking to provide "hands-on" support. The occupational angel usually has up to £50,000 to invest – often as a result of a redundancy payment – and is seeking full-time employment within the business.

It is worth noting that, in many cases, the additional experience that an angel can bring may be just as beneficial as the equity they invest. New skills can help the business to grow beyond your original plans and the ability to use your angel as a sounding board - bouncing ideas based on his or her experience - can be invaluable.

It is important to remember that Business Angels invest in only a very small proportion of the businesses they see; typically, at least seven out of eight opportunities are rejected.

The Business Angel will want to investigate the business concept thoroughly before agreeing to invest and, in all cases, will be seeking an equity stake in the business and usually a clear exit route. They will want to know when, and at what price, you expect to be able to buy them out.

In all cases, be it patron, entrepreneurial or occupational, the angel will be looking for tax reliefs on their investment and Enterprise Investment Scheme relief is particularly important in this context.

PRIVATE EQUITY

For investment levels over £1m, institutional private equity can often be the best option. The UK private equity market can currently be characterized as "too much money chasing too few deals." There are a lot of providers looking for good opportunities in which to invest their money. However, this does not mean that it is a private equity seeker's market. Venture capitalists look for a high return on their investment and will expect demanding targets from the companies in which they invest.

There are hundreds of private equity providers that seek to differentiate themselves by deal size and type or business sector. The key is to chose the right private equity partner for your particular business circumstances. Your funder should bring more than just money. If they are a sector specialist they will have a knowledge of your industry that will be useful. All will have experience in how to realise their - and your - investment. And they will have a specific interest in growing your business quickly - so they should be coming to you with ideas and opportunities.

Throughout the fund-raising process make sure that you meet and work with the individuals within the private equity institution who will ultimately be responsible for the investment in your business. After all, by definition, private equity is private.

Once you have chosen your partner you will be stuck with them until they realise their equity stake. Furthermore, as a shareholder you can expect restrictions on when you can transfer your shares and to whom. However, since the private equity investor will be seeking an exit for his money, your business will become focused on this which, potentially, will benefit all shareholders.

Many institutions are flexible and will consider investing in a business just to allow existing shareholders to realise some of their holding. The decision by a private equity provider to invest in your business is taken on a purely commercial basis, although some have their own guidelines. For example, some will not invest in start-ups or specific business sectors and others have limits on the amounts they can invest. However, the business must have regular and reliable management information and due diligence checks will be undertaken on your business as part of the investment process.

Private equity players all have their own particular areas of emphasis which they will take into consideration before agreeing to invest. These include a growing market, ability to maintain a competitive edge and strong growth opportunities. They will also be looking for a strong focus on management. The management team's track record will be investigated and those teams who can demonstrate that they have done it before will be sought.

The eventual exit will also be a critical factor. Private equity investors will be seeking to realise their investment at a substantial profit within a particular timescale.

As a rule of thumb, you will be expected to make a strong case for how your business can double its value over three years. In summary, to secure private equity you will be required to show that a substantial capital gain can be achieved (for all shareholders) and that you are the right management team to deliver it.

If neither business angels nor private equity finance is suitable

- or if you are looking to further expand the business having already used one of these options - then flotation is probably the next route to consider.

Determining whether or not your company should go public is probably one of the most significant decisions you and your fellow shareholders will have to make. Having made the decision, however, you must then consider which market to choose.

GOING PUBLIC

Until recently a listing on the main London Stock Exchange was the only viable option. However, today there are a number of smaller markets open to business, the Alternative Investment Market (AIM) being one of the most relevant.

AIM is the junior market of the London Stock Exchange and, although part of the Exchange, is specifically designed to operate and be regulated separately from the main market. It was introduced in June 1995 to allow those smaller growth-orientated companies that are unable to meet the strict criteria for full listing to take advantage of the facilities offered by the Exchange to raise capital and trade shares.

There are no set requirements for the size of company being admitted, history of trading or percentage of shares in public hands. However, companies seeking an AIM listing will need to demonstrate established financial control procedures and it is important that directors understand and accept their responsibilities.

Most listings on AIM fall into a market capitalisation range of £1m to £10m. Below £1m, costs take up a disproportionate part of the funds raised – and above £10m – full listing may well be more suitable, although there are a number of admission criteria and tax reasons for preferring AIM.

As an AIM-listed company you will have a nominated adviser, called a Nomad, who will expect you to follow the corporate governance procedures (the Combined code). The Model Code for directors share dealings will also apply. The Nomad is the company's point of contact with the Exchange. and will make all the decisions on suitability and other regulatory matters for AIM companies. Nomads can only be appointed by the Exchange and their performance is regularly checked against a strict set of rules – indeed it is more difficult to be authorised to act as a Nomad than to sponsor a company for a full listing.

AIM is a development capital market in that it is used primarily to raise money to grow a business rather than to payout existing shareholders. It has only been in existence for a short time and, to a certain extent therefore, is untested. However, it does represent an important opportunity for smaller companies to raise capital and unlock shareholding value in a way that was not possible before its creation.

In contrast to AIM, full listing on the main market demands strict admission criteria which is set out in the London Stock Exchange's Listing Rules, otherwise known as the Yellow Book. In particular you need to demonstrate:

- *A three-year track record of trading and revenue earning, evidenced in audited accounts with the latest audited figures being no more than six months old at the time of listing;*

- *Directors and senior management team who can prove they have appropriate collective experience and expertise to run all areas of the business; and*

- *Strong financial and operating controls.*

In addition, 25 per cent of the shares being listed must be in the hands of the public and the company must publish a comprehensive prospectus including financial information and appoint a "sponsor" to ensure compliance with the Stock Exchange's listings.

Because of the significant professional fees involved, it is important that sufficient monies are raised through the flotation to make the exercise worthwhile. Most companies joining the main market are capitalised at £20m or more, although a lower capitalisation may be acceptable, depending on the circumstances.

The main benefits for pursuing a listing on the Stock Exchange are that it provides access to capital for growth; liquidity of investment by providing a market for trading in the shares; and increased public profile and credibility. Your customers and suppliers can have confidence in your business because you operate within a strict regulatory framework. It is also easier to implement employee share incentive schemes and corporate governance can lead to efficiency savings. On the reverse side of the coin, however, your shares have a market and anyone can buy them, leading to a potential loss of control or a takeover by an unwelcome acquirer.

The pressure to manage share-price performance in the short term may not always lead to sensible long-term decision-making, and the high public profile might not be good when things are going wrong. Remember too, it is the small company that often fails to reap the benefits of a full listing. Last year small companies underperformed in the market across all sectors, so think twice before pursuing a listing and always seek advice on the likely market appetite for businesses like yours.

In summary therefore, the options for equity finance are varied – ranging from business angels at one end of the scale through to full listing. There are also overseas options such as NASDAQ (the US capital market) and EASDAQ (the European capital market).

Each option has its own particular considerations, but at the end of the day, raising equity via any of these routes is all about convincing someone that their investment will be worth substantially more in the future than it is when they invest.

Whatever your rationale for choosing to raise equity finance it is critical that you have a clear strategy to take your business forward: the more an equity investor believes in your opportunity, the better the deal for you.

A detailed analysis of your own aspirations and those of the business is critical. Examine your business, your market, your management strengths – and weaknesses – and put together a detailed business plan explaining what you are going to achieve and how you are gong to get there. Raising equity can lead to substantial growth and enhancement in shareholder value. However, the process needs to be carefully handled to make sure that you get the best deal for you and your business.

CASE STUDY

Jewel is a company that designs, imports and distributes costume jewellery – rings, necklaces, bracelets and brooches retailing for under £30. Goods are manufactured in the Far East and sold to independent retailers and high street multiples in the UK. The product offering includes own-label products and a range of branded goods.

The business has grown very quickly. Over a recent four-year period, turnover increased from £2m to £11m and operating profit rose from £400,000 to nearly £3m.

Alan White, Jewel's owner and managing director who had been responsible for the company's strong growth, was conscious of the sizable value that the business had built up and wanted to realise some of his wealth.

Initially, he felt that his best option was to sell the business, effectively cashing in on his efforts to date. A sale would have made him enough money never to have to work again. However, he was not entirely comfortable with this strategy as he was not ready to retire and he strongly believed in Jewel's future. The prospects for the business were excellent. Opportunities existed to expand sales into Europe and the US and to widen the product range. But to exploit these opportunities the management team needed strengthening. Although able to take the business forward, the steps required were making White a little nervous.

He decided to market the business to a limited number of parties, with two possible outcomes: sale of the whole business to a trade buyer; or a fund-raising, via a sale of some of the shares to a funding institution or using debt, to allow White, the major shareholder, to realise some funds.

Attractive offers from UK equity providers and banks, and from companies, were received. One downside in relation to a trade sale was that to secure the best price, White would have had to remain working within the business for up to two years. The prospect of "having a boss" was not attractive to him, despite the money.

In the end, he chose to sell 25 per cent of the business to a UK institution for £4.5m – an all-equity solution, because the business had never had substantial debt levels and White was unwilling to place any additional financial risk on his shareholding. As part of the deal, White – still the major shareholder – developed a strategic plan demonstrating how Jewel could exploit future opportunities. Two non-executive directors were introduced to the business who could help him to recruit the right people into the company and plan for a full successful exit for all the shareholders in the medium term.

Chapter 8

Growth through acquisition

Sometimes the only way to achieve rapid growth is to acquire an existing business as Stephen Baker, head of corporate finance at Grant Thornton, explains

There are many reasons for buying a business...it can increase buying power with suppliers or enable you to acquire a distribution network for an existing product line. It can achieve consolidation of supply or of markets, and it can help reduce risk through product diversification. Whatever the underlying reasons, the one thing all acquisition strategies have in common is a desire to strengthen and grow the existing business.

Figures collated in the *1999 Grant Thornton European Business Survey* reveal that nearly half the UK SMEs who anticipate a change in business ownership expect it to be via a trade sale...so there should be ample opportunity for acquisition. The question is how do you go about it?

CONDUCTING A REVIEW

The first step is to review your existing business to assess your motives for making an acquisition and to identify your own strengths, skills and resources. This review will reveal if an acquisition is the best option and whether there are obstacles or shortcomings in the existing business which could prevent a successful combination. Take, for example, a sales-orientated organisation which chooses to acquire a supplier in order to reduce costs with the objective of increasing profits. If the existing management has no experience of operating a factory the acquired business can quickly spiral out of control.

Once you have established that growth through acquisition

represents a viable option, the next step is to define the search criteria for an acquisition target. In some instances targets may be obvious. For example, a strategy to add markets to the core business will lead a purchaser to acquire the strongest competitors in regions where it is weak. On the other hand, a strategy of product diversification opens a broad choice of potential businesses.

Some acquisitions can be opportunistic, for example, when a suitable target goes into receivership. Businesses seeking growth through acquisition should always be alert to this type of opportunity. Others can be undertaken on an ad hoc basis, by subscribing to commercial networks which advertise businesses for sale. However, while these approaches can generate positive results, the most effective method of acquisition is carefully planned target research which professional advisers will be able to advise on. When seeking targets, potential acquirers and their advisers must plan how much time and resource they are prepared to apply to research – some information is cheap and easy to access while other data is priced at premium level. You will need to decide how useful it is and how much you are prepared to pay for it.

Research can reveal or confirm industry projections; market trends; transactions by specific businesses; key players in a market; the ownership structure of the business and the valuations of similar businesses. The key to how useful it will be is creativity and the ability to think "outside the box" in identifying opportunities.

MAKING AN APPROACH TO THE TARGET

After one or more targets has been identified an approach must then be made to the target/targets to discover whether they are interested in a deal. At this stage confidentiality is of the utmost importance and a suitor will often have to sign a confidentiality agreement if they wish to pursue the opportunity.

Negotiations must be flexible. Information will be shared which raises points for agreement, discussion or renegotiation. It is important, therefore, to remember that the final aim is always completion – too often this can be delayed unnecessarily by lack of deal management and planning.

Tactics will depend primarily on whether or not the target is attractive to competing bidders. However, in most cases, the first stage of negotiation will be to set out the principal terms upon which you wish to deal. This is known as an offer letter and usually becomes a base document for forthcoming negotiations.

The offer letter should whet the appetite of a vendor and should contain an indicative offer price; outline the nature of consideration including any earnout or deferred consideration; and state any desired tax structure.

EXCLUSIVITY

At the earliest possible stage in negotiations the purchaser should seek exclusivity. This is achieved by means of a "lockout" clause which may be agreed as early as the initial approach, but is typically not secured until after the initial offer letter has been received. The lockout ensures that the vendor does not negotiate with any other parties for a given period, thereby giving both parties the time to complete the sale and purchase agreement. In order to be enforceable, the lockout agreement must be for a fixed period and be made under seal.

In certain cases it may be appropriate for the purchaser to include provisions for cost considerations where the exclusivity period is breached. It is also common for the vendor to seek evidence of finance by a given date and, in such circumstances, exclusivity can be a two stage process with evidence of finance required by a given date followed by a further lockout period to conclude the transaction. When structuring a deal, the purchaser is likely to have three key objectives:

■ *To reduce the price;*

■ *To reduce the funding requirement or structure it in the most convenient way; and*

■ *To structure the transaction in the most tax-efficient manner.*

Although tax structuring is often driven by the vendor's circumstances, tax benefits can be shared between the two parties through careful negotiations. The vendor will be seeking to obtain maximum profit for his enterprise and will often attempt to make the business as attractive as possible. The purchaser should therefore seek to differentiate between genuine recurring benefits and short-term "window dressing" which can include temporary reductions in capital expenditure investment, marketing and other discretionary expenditure.

The purchaser will need to think carefully about what is being bought. Does he intend to merge his existing business with the new acquisition or run them separately? Deal structure starts with the commercial logic of the combination, not with tax or financial considerations. Decide which companies or business entities are wanted. It may be, for example, that the vendor's premises are not required. In this instance it could make sense to leave these out of the deal, thereby potentially increasing the overall ability for the vendor to raise extra monies without any financial implication falling on the purchaser.

The purchaser should also carry out a detailed review of the working capital requirement. For example, there are often big reductions to be had by clearing out the warehouse and reducing the amount of stock held.

TUPE

One misconception of purchasers, particularly in an asset sale, is that they can leave behind unwanted employees. However, all employees are covered by the Transfer of Undertakings (Protection of Employment) Regulations 1981 and, as a consequence, if the business is transferred as a going concern and classified as an "undertaking", they will automatically become employed by the purchaser. In addition, their accrued rights and claims and the terms and conditions of employment will also pass to the purchaser.

As many business acquisitions lead to a rationalisation of the workforce it is essential that the purchaser quantifies the total contingent liability prior to finalising the deal, including pension benefits of the new company. The purchaser should also insist on warranties and indemnities with respect to employee claims and attaching contingent liabilities. It is also worth noting that as purchaser you may have to negotiate with other parties in addition to the vendor. Requirements of senior directors and key employees who may or may not have shareholding, will have to be met. Any non-competition clauses will need to be agreed. Another potential dealbreaker is the requirement of a main supplier, who may not agree to you acting as its agents or may choose to negotiate new terms. Where rented premises are involved, a landlord may not consent to a transfer of the lease if the covenant of the tenant is weakened.

PROFESSIONAL ADVICE

These are all time-consuming tasks and are best handled on your behalf by your professional advisers. At all stages of the deal process it is important that you don't lose sight of the aims and needs of the core business...neglect at this stage could seriously hamper the success of the deal. In addition, your adviser should be a skilled negotiator who is aware of the issues likely to arise. Provided you have regular briefing and debriefing sessions you will be able to keep up to speed with the deal without sacrificing the energies you need to spend on your existing business.

At the end of the day, what you need to remember is that you are making an investment, often substantial, in a target business. You need to get what you think you are buying without paying too much for it.

Entrepreneurs must always look forward with vision to meet the challenges of changing markets, competition and regulations. Businesses are bought – and sold – in anticipation of these changes or in reaction to them. A successful acquisition is based on clear business strategies aimed at producing real growth in value.

Chapter 9

Tax management

Robert Purry, head of tax at Grant Thornton, assesses the core taxes of which any growing company should be aware

The financial structure of a growing company requires careful deliberation, not only in terms of whether it should use debt, equity or a combination of the two, but also over which is the most tax efficient. Tax planning can be used to make possible a deal which otherwise may not have been viable.

Further, when raising finance, you should also consider methods for incentivising staff. After all, in periods of growth, businesses rely on their staff to help its development. However, pay rises are often not given due to the need to invest all available profits back into the business for continued growth.

It is therefore necessary to formulate the company's policy from the outset, particularly as the reward mechanism may involve providing equity. This can be done in various ways, such as providing equity directly, phantom shares or the use of an employee share incentive scheme. However, different incentive schemes have different tax implications and, normally, a combination of the schemes best suits a company to enable it to meet the needs of all its employees.

RAISING FINANCE
To encourage investment in private companies there are two schemes available which incentivise investors by providing tax breaks. These are the Enterprise Investment Scheme (EIS) and Venture Capital Trusts (VCT).

Enterprise Investment Scheme (EIS)
The purpose of the EIS is to assist certain types of businesses to raise capital. This is done by providing a range of tax reliefs for

investors in qualifying shares in these companies. The businesses which qualify are unquoted trading companies with gross assets prior to EIS investment of £15m or less. For EIS purposes, a listing on AIM is treated as unquoted. In addition, the company must be involved in a qualifying trade. This is broadly all forms of trading excluding land dealing, financial activities, legal/accountancy services and property-backed activities. The money raised through the EIS must be used by the company within 12 months of the share issue or, in the case of a new business, within 12 months of the company starting to trade.

Both income tax and capital gains tax reliefs are available to the investor subject to various conditions being satisfied. These include not being connected to the company being invested in (eg. by employment, partnership or an associate of one), or owning more than 30 per cent of the share capital, loan capital or having control over more than 30 per cent of the voting rights. The investor must satisfy these conditions for two years before and five years after the issue of the shares. The tax reliefs available are 20 per cent income tax relief on a maximum investment of £150,000 and no capital gains tax on the disposal of the EIS shares, provided they are held for at least five years from the date of issue. Other capital gains can also be deferred until the EIS shares are sold.

Venture Capital Trusts (VCT)

A VCT is a quoted company which invests shareholders' funds in smaller, unquoted (including AIM) trading companies which have a potential for growth. Both income tax and capital gains tax benefits are available on investments up to £100,000. For a company to benefit from an investment by a VCT it can not have gross assets prior to investment of £15m nor can it receive more than £1m each year from a VCT. In addition, a VCT cannot hold more than 15 per cent of its value in one company. For an individual investing in a VCT, 20 per cent income tax relief is available and capital gains tax is not payable on VCT shares when sold, provided the shares have been held for five years. As with EIS, other capital gains can be deferred until the VCT shares are sold.

SHARE INCENTIVE SCHEMES

Share incentive schemes also known as share option schemes, enable a company to give employees the right to buy shares in the company at a fixed price during a specific period. There are, however, considerable differences between an approved and unapproved scheme.

Membership of an approved scheme does not have to involve all employees and can be restricted to specific groups and directors if required.

The initial cash flow benefit of such a scheme is that no income tax is payable at the grant or exercise of the option, unless certain conditions are broken. Thereafter capital gains tax (CGT) is charged on the subsequent sale of the shares but the annual CGT exemption can be utilised if not used elsewhere. CGT taper relief may also be available but the period for taper relief will only commence when the option is exercised, not granted.

The value of the shares over which an individual has options under an approved share option scheme must not exceed £30,000 at the time the options are granted.

The tax breaks for unapproved schemes are not as attractive, although unlike approved share option schemes, all employees are eligible to join, even shareholders who have a 10 per cent stake in the company. Employees are not taxed on the grant of the option unless the option can be exercised more than ten years after it was granted.

On exercise an income tax charge arises on the difference between the market value of the shares and the exercise price. In addition, options granted after 6 April 1999 will be liable to employers national insurance. The rate of national insurance is that in force when the option is exercised.

A capital gains tax charge arises on the sale of the shares on the difference between sale proceeds and the market value when the option was exercised. The gain may attract CGT taper relief if the option was exercised at least three years prior to sale.

The downside to unapproved schemes is the tax charge that arises on the employee and the national insurance charge on the employer when the option is exercised. The employee can be saddled with a tax charge without receiving any cash benefit and shares received through such schemes may be difficult to sell in a private company because of the lack of marketability, unless an EBT (Employee Benefit Trust) is set up to provide a market.

An alternative may be a Save As You Earn (SAYE) Share Option Scheme, in particular for lower paid employees. These schemes require Inland Revenue approval and must be open to all employees who have served a chosen qualifying period.

SAYE options may be granted at a discount of up to 20 per cent of market value at the time of grant. Employees can save between £5 and £250 per month for either three, five or seven years. At the end of this period the proceeds of the savings contracts can be used to fund the acquisition of shares (or the employee can take the proceeds in cash).

While the amount which can be set aside to buy the shares is comparatively low, this type of scheme can be very effective in spreading share ownership throughout the workforce.

No tax liability arises on the employee when the option is granted or exercised and there will only be a liability to CGT if the shares are subsequently sold for a profit. The interest earned on the savings contract and any terminal bonus received are also exempt from income tax.

The use of share schemes often raises the following two questions: How do the employees sell their shares? How do I keep control of my business if I am giving shares away? These are considered below.

Creation of a market – using an Employee Benefit Trust (EBT)

Creation of a market to enable employees to sell their shares can be achieved by using an employee benefit trust (EBT). The trust can be used to buy shares from employees who leave and then hold them until another individual wants shares. This means that the company does not have to use its own funds to buy the shares direct, provided there are sufficient funds held within the EBT - leaving the company's funds available to be used more

Find out how Grant Thornton can help your business grow

Do you want to work with a firm which:

■ is committed to providing comprehensive and relevant advice
■ works with clients – not just for them
■ has 42 offices throughout the UK and is part of a global network with representation in over 90 countries?

If the answer is YES then Grant Thornton is the solution.

For a free consultation to find out more about how we can help your business, **complete this postcard (no stamp necessary)**, **call us on 020 7728 2758** or **e-mail melanie.tibbert@gtuk.com**. Alternatively, visit our website at www.grant-thornton.co.uk.

Please tick here if you would like a:
☐ **Free consultation**

If you would like more information on any of our core services, please tick the appropriate boxes:
☐ **Audit**
☐ **Business advisory services**
☐ **Corporate finance**
☐ **Forensic and litigation support**
☐ **Going public**
☐ **PRIMA® – People and Relationship Issues in Management**
☐ **Recovery and Reorganisation**
☐ **UK and international tax services**

Name

Position

Company name

Address

Postcode   Telephone

Fax   E-mail

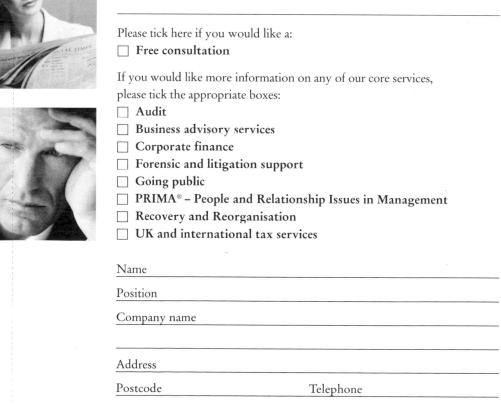

MELANIE TIBBERT
GRANT THORNTON
(NATIONAL MARKETING)
GRANT THORNTON HOUSE
MELTON STREET
EUSTON SQUARE
LONDON
NW1 0YW

effectively elsewhere. Financial assistance can, however, be given by the company if needed.

Any contributions made by the company to an EBT may qualify for corporation tax relief. If they are considered of a regular and a revenue nature, the potential beneficiaries of the EBT are limited to employees of the company (with the possible addition of a charity if the trust has to be wound up) and no contributions can be returned to the company.

An alternative to a share option scheme – a phantom share scheme

A phantom share scheme allows employees to benefit from the growth in value of the company but without the main shareholders diluting their shareholding, as would be the case with approved or unapproved schemes.

Under this arrangement, employees receive bonuses taxable as normal salary and potentially liable to national insurance.

The bonus is calculated by a formula tailored to meet the company's requirements. The formula can include, for example, the level of annual profits over a certain threshold, the growth in share value over a financial year or the dividend paid to ordinary shareholders. Schemes can also provide for a second bonus to be paid if the company is sold or perhaps floated.

The annual amount enables employees who participate in the scheme to receive an annual payment (akin to a dividend for shareholders) and the second bonus provides a reward on any sale/flotation (akin to a capital gain for shareholders).

A "phantom" scheme has the distinct advantage of not being governed by any legislation other than the general Schedule E rules, and employers can target such employees as they may wish. These schemes are therefore attractive to private companies and their employees for a number of reasons. Employees can join the scheme without having to meet a tax bill when no cash has actually been received, the employer receiving a corporation tax deduction for any "notional dividend" paid out, which would not be available if it were a dividend on "real shares". The main shareholders do not dilute their shareholdings. The new proposed share schemes, outlined below, may change the position but at present phantom share schemes are currently the most popular way for employers to incentivise their staff, whether it be for continued growth, or preparing a company for sale/flotation.

However, as the case studies opposite show, a phantom share scheme is not always the answer.

NEW SHARE SCHEMES

Following the 1999 Budget, the Inland Revenue intends to introduce new tax reliefs for key personnel which will apply to awards in the form of free or cheap shares, convertible shares and "long-term incentive plans". These tie the award of the shares to such conditions as the individual remaining with the company.

The "Enterprise Management Incentives" (EMI) enables a company to attract a limited number, six has been suggested, of employees. The initial limit is likely to be capped at £100,000 which is more favourable than the current limit of £30,000 on approved share schemes (see above). Unlike existing unapproved share schemes, a tax charge (to CGT) would only arise on the sale of the shares and under the proposals there would be no national insurance charge. With the increase in employer's national insurance the scheme could give a big cash advantage. If additional remuneration was paid instead, this would be liable to both employer's national insurance and PAYE. The Budget also announced plans for a new all employee share scheme. The main proposals enable employees to allocate up to £1,500 of salary (tax and national insurance deferred) to buy shares (partnership shares). In addition, the company can give twice the amount of shares bought (free matching shares) and up to a further £3,000 of shares (completely free shares) to an employee. All shares would be held by a trust.

A corporation tax deduction is given for salary allocated to partnership shares, the value of the free shares and costs of setting up and running the scheme. Both schemes are expected to start in 2000 but the final regulations need to be published before it is determined how the schemes will work in practice.

CASE STUDIES

The following case studies are real life situations where some form of share incentive scheme was implemented.

CASE STUDY A

Internet Link Limited is an IT company looking to float on AIM in the next couple of years. However, the problem the directors had was how to retain its staff, as they were, as with most IT firms, the reason for its success.

Accordingly, both an approved and unapproved share option scheme were put in place, with options being linked to performance. The unapproved scheme had certain of its directors/shareholders as members which enabled the management team as well as the IT specialists to be given an incentive to assist the performance of the company for its AIM flotation. With the AIM flotation imminent, the market was already in place.

CASE STUDY B

For Software Solutions and Millar's Engineering Limited a phantom share scheme was preferred to a conventional share option scheme – but for different reasons.

Software Solutions, another computer company, used the phantom share scheme as it did not have sufficient cash at the time it wanted to pay bonuses to the staff.

However, Millar's Engineering had a more intricate problem having given two of its employees 10 per cent and 9 per cent of its share capital in its early days. These employees had left the company but refused to give/sell the shares back. The company, while wanting to use some means of profit-sharing for its staff, did not want a repeat of this. A phantom scheme was therefore implemented.

SUMMARY

Both the EIS and VCIs can generate valuable cash for a company. Each type of scheme could provide up to £1m of funds for use by a company, for qualifying purposes, and often provides that additional incentive to investors.

However, just as importantly, share schemes are a good way of incentivising employees and also provide a way of tackling one of the current Government's tasks of "promoting enterprise for all and increasing productivity". If structured appropriately, they can also provide valuable cash flow benefits to the company, leaving what funds are available for reinvestment. Exactly which scheme suits a company depends on the individual circumstances and its plans for the future.

Chapter 10

Living in the fast lane

Claire Oldfield, Sunday Times Business Correspondent, takes a look at some of the fast-growth success stories and how they were financed

In 1990 Roger Keenan came up with an idea to develop a business based around digital voice-recording technology. At the time he was a 26-year-old engineer, without a financial or management background, and his office was in his garage. His inexperience showed as his success in raising money from venture capitalists - to transform his business plan into a reality - amounted to be zero.

EYRETEL

But Keenan saw the potential in his venture and was determined that it would grow beyond his garage. He managed to get a £70,000 loan from NatWest and £155,000 from business angels and then secured his first order from the US state of Virginia. After that Eyretel began to grow stratospherically: sales soared by 215 per cent over three years and today Keenan runs one of the country's fastest-growing businesses, as measured by the *Sunday Times/Virgin Atlantic Fast Track 100* league table of fast-growing unquoted firms.

In 1998 Keenan finally secured the elusive venture capital backing, with a £22.5m injection from Apax Partners to grow the company further.

DX COMMUNICATIONS

At the same time as Keenan was growing Eyretel, Richard Emanuel was selling cellular phones door-to-door in Glasgow. He funded his start-up with £1,300 of savings and a £3,000 bank overdraft. By 1996 it was clear that Emanuel was on to a winning formula with DX Communications, the mobile phone retailer, and he sold a 26 per cent stake to Cellnet to boost expansion. By October 1998 his company had more than 100 stores, with combined sales of £37m, and 700 employees.

What both these stories illustrate is the long-held view that financing a start-up is hard work, is often done on a shoestring and usually involves a high degree of personal risk.

In contrast, the perceived view is that financing growth – once you have proved that your product sells and gained the confidence of potential backers – is the easy bit, especially because the growth of small firms is where future jobs and economic growth are going to come from. Think again. Financing growth is harder than it seems.

STAYING FOCUSED

Keenan and Emanuel have made the growth of their companies look almost effortless, but part of their success has come because they were focused from the outset on where they wanted to take their businesses. They are both risk-takers who believed in their business and were prepared to fly by the seat of their pants for a while until their enterprise delivered results.

These qualities are common among all entrepreneurs who grow their ventures beyond a one-man-band into a business of substance.

But not all entrepreneurs manage to achieve such impressive growth, nor do they persevere to seek out the most appropriate financing method for their particular business. Thousands struggle in vain to find venture capitalists or business angels who are sufficiently confident in their enterprise to fund expansion, and in the end turn to more conventional financing.

For instance, there are still entrepreneurs who put their house up as collateral or fund entire ventures through their credit cards. Others turn to even more desperate measures to ensure that their venture grows and simply withhold payment to customers and suppliers until the last minute so that the maximum amount of cash remains in the business. Many others forgo profit to ensure that sales are high.

MBI MBO

But for some entrepreneurs conventional borrowing is sufficient to finance growth. Take Bryan Duffy, who financed MBI MBO, his hotel business, through a long-term bank loan secured against the property. So far it has returned almost 50 per cent of its original capital.

Other entrepreneurs who are fixed on growth opt for factoring, whereby all their debts are chased by a third party so that they can concentrate on growing their business. Cris Howarth at Bon Bon Buddies, a confectioner, is strongly in favour of factoring. "Without factoring, Bon Bon Buddies would no longer be in business because of the seasonality of the chocolate market," he says. Factoring is perfect for companies like this, with good internal accounting and a blue-chip client list.

But the best way to finance the growth of an enterprise is often to get backing from individuals – business angels – who are prepared to risk some of their own cash to fund expansion. Angels usually invest "spare" cash and so do not rely heavily on the investment coming good – for them part of the thrill of the investment is the risk element.

Sometimes the risk pays off. Keenan got a £20,000 investment in 1992 from a retired couple, who saw the value of their holding increase to £3m when Apax invested. And perhaps the best-known example of a business angel who made a shrewd investment is that of Ian McGlinn. He is the man who put up £4,000 in 1976 so that Anita Roddick could roll out her Body Shop concept. The value of his stake soared and he remains the largest individual shareholder in the business.

EAT

Other entrepreneurs go one step further and recognise that the only way to grow rapidly is to get a serious injection of capital and expertise. These are the people who seek out venture capitalists. Niall MacArthur began his chain of sandwich shops, called Eat, just three years ago. From the start he was focused on going for growth. He already has seven cafes in the London area, has the sites to double this figure by the end of the year, and plans to have expanded to 30 outlets by 2001. But the price he paid to grow so quickly was high: he sacrificed 40 per cent of his equity in Eat in return for cash from venture capitalists, 3i.

FIRST TELECOM

Similarly, Marc Citron, who founded First Telecom, has swapped over 30 per cent of his firm's equity in return for a cash injection from Morgan Stanley Capital Partners, to drive growth of the telecom firm on the Continent.

Even though they end up giving away some of the company they have built up, entrepreneurs who succeed in getting venture-capital backing remain in the minority. This is perhaps best illustrated through the Fast Trackers: just over 20 per cent of the 1998 list of the fastest-growing firms in the UK used venture capital to grow. In contrast, about 80 per cent relied on internal funding, about 35 per cent used short-term debt and almost 30 per cent used factoring to finance growth.

Financing growth is trickier than it seems. Take those company founders who have not dared to take on more staff, even though they have more work than they can handle, simply because they do not have the confidence to do so. Or those who overestimate the number of customers they will have and borrow money on the strength of it - only to come crashing to the ground when their company goes belly-up.

ARM HOLDINGS

Most of the real growth successes come not from the type of finance used, but the way it is used and the focus of the individuals involved.

Take ARM Holdings, which became the first billion-pound IT company to be listed on the London stock market. ARM began life as a joint venture between Acorn and Apple, who each invested £1.5m and saw it soar to a value of hundreds of millions of pounds. From the outset Robin Saxby, who heads the company, knew that there was a huge market for a chipless chip maker and had the confidence that came from his big-name backers.

But Saxby was lucky in his financing. Other entrepreneurs have to rely on banks, which tend to be cautious about financing high-tech companies – such as Internet companies – with few conventional assets or profits in their early phase.

LINK LICENSING AND BODEN

Although the fastest growth tends to come from the telecoms and high-tech sectors, there are other industries that also have dynamic growth stories to tell. Take Claire Derry at Link Licensing and Johnnie Boden at his mail-order clothing firm, who have both grown their ventures. Derry had venture capital backing to buy Link from United Newspapers and with the deal came free office space, which enabled her to grow the company. Boden, who spent a rocky couple of years building his mail-order firm, enlisting his friends to model for the Boden catalogues.

GEMSTONE TRAVEL

But my favourite financing story is that of Gemstone Travel, which was launched in 1993 after the founders secured a home-improvement loan from Marks & Spencer. The founders still maintain that Marks & Spencer thinks the cash went to renovate a kitchen rather than build a multi-million-pound business.

So what do all these case histories tell us about financing growth in UK? Certainly there are enough entrepreneurs out there willing to take risks, and certainly there is enough finance to allow them to do so. But the two things do not always come together to enable new enterprises to be grown into businesses of substance. And, despite all the financial options available, there is no doubt that the major source of backing to finance growth is still internal - which suggests that there is much that could be done to improve the chances of success for fast-growth firms.

If this all sounds rather bleak, consider the following statistic: just 4 per cent of the American Inc 500 (a US league table of up-and-coming fast-growth firms) have received venture capital to finance their growth. So perhaps the spirit of enterprise is flourishing in the UK after all.

BUSINESS FINANCE: SOME FACTS AND FIGURES

Earlier this year the IoD conducted a survey of its members into sources of business finance. Below, Richard Wilson, IoD business research executive, presents the results

Business finance may seem a somewhat prosaic subject, but it is an issue of crucial importance to the UK business community. Enterprises need a ready supply of capital to finance their day-to-day activities, exploit market opportunities and enhance their competitive edge. The provision of finance is of particular concern for small and medium-sized enterprises (SMEs).

SMEs make a major contribution to innovation, employment and competition. If the SME sector is to prosper, it must have access to adequate sources of capital. However, since the publication of the MacMillan Report in 1931 there has been a continuing debate over whether small firms find it unduly difficult to secure long-term finance. This discussion has been given a new lease of life following the publication of the Government's Competitiveness White Paper, the decision by the Chancellor of the Exchequer, Gordon Brown, to ask Don Cruickshank to carry out an investigation of the banking sector, and recent research by the Bank of England.

Respondents to the IoD's survey numbered 1,331 members, as profiled below:

Respondents by firm size	%
Micro-firms (ie. firms with fewer than 9 employees)	30
Small businesses (ie. firms with between 10-49 employees)	39
Medium-sized enterprises (ie. firms with between 20-249 employees)	24
Large companies (ie. firms with over 250 employees)	8

Respondents by industry	%
Business/professional services	36
Distribution/retail	12
Financial services	4
Government, education, health and personal services	3
Manufacturing	17
High/new technology (eg. IT, biotechnology, etc.)	13
Other (including construction, mining and transport)	17

The main sources of finance

A business's choice of finance is of considerable importance because it can have an impact on its future growth. Other things being equal, a firm that relies extensively on bank overdraft financing, for example, is likely to be potentially vulnerable in an economic down turn.

The table below shows how those IoD members who participated in the survey have financed their business activities over the past five years. (Throughout the survey, respondents could select as many of these categories as they deemed appropriate.)

How have you financed your firm's activities over the last five years?	%
Investment of capital by owner(s)/director(s)/shareholders	63
Retained profits	74
Revenue from sales	47
Trade creditors	18
Bank (or other institution) overdraft	54
Bank (or other institution) loan	35
Loan by owner(s)/director(s)	28
Family	6
Leasing	20

How have you financed your firm's activities over the last five years?	%
Factoring	7
Venture capital	5
Business angel	2
Loan Guarantee Scheme	5
Stock exchange flotation	2
Other	5

Purpose of raising external finance

Seventy-nine per cent of respondents sought external capital to finance their business operations. The table below summarises their purpose in seeking it.

If you have used external finance, what was the primary reason	%
Sales on credit/stock/working capital	49
Equipment	55
Land/buildings	28
Additional personnel	13
Staff training	7
Marketing	15
Export promotion	5
Research and development/new product development	17
To cover financial losses	13
Other	11

Factors influencing the choice of finance

In theory, firms have a considerable variety of different sources of external finance from which to choose. Of the 1,084 respondents who explained what determined their choice, the majority stated that cost was the principal influencing factor. For almost half, however, the existence of a previous good relationship with a source of capital was a key determining factor. Evidently, many respondents prefer to stick with the devil they know, rather than take a risk and approach a new provider of capital.

What determines your choice of external finance?	%
Cost	72
Speed with which finance can be obtained	39
No requirement for personal collateral	45
Previous good experience with source of finance	47
Maintenance of business control	41
Advice of bank/accountant/consultant	26
Other	6

Indirect benefits of raising external finance

Of those respondents who raised external finance, 71 per cent claimed that they had not experienced any indirect benefits as a result of this activity.

Those respondents who acknowledged that they had gained indirect advantages from raising external finance, described the following benefits.

What indirect benefits did you gain from raising external finance	%
Increased access to advice on finance	47
It made me provide better financial information	45
Greater awareness of the need to monitor cash flow	63
Other	21

Range of external finance available

Of those who expressed an opinion on the range of external finance available, 69 per cent stated that they were happy with the choice of options available to them. This reflects the increasing range of financial products available to many firms and an economic climate that is relatively favourable to borrowers.

Advice and information about finance

Of those members who revealed where they sought financial information and advice, the vast majority looked to their accountant and bank:

Where do you seek information and advice about sources of finance	%
Bank	75
Chamber of Commerce	7
Business Link	17
TEC	5
Trade association	6
Financial press	23
Enterprise agency	3
Accountant/professional adviser	79
Factoring/invoice discounting company	8
Leasing company	14
Business contact	30
Family	6
Others	8

Equity finance

One of the most significant findings of the survey was a high level of support for equity finance. 51 per cent of respondents stated that they were prepared in principle to consider the sale of shares in their business. This stands in marked contrast to some other surveys on small business finance.

The relationship between businesses and their banks

Another important finding of the survey was that, generally speaking, respondents had a good relationship with their banks. 73 per cent described their relationship with their bank as good and only 5 per cent considered that they had a bad relationship with their bank.

Respondents' experience of lending conditions over the past year was somewhat mixed. 41 per cent did not feel that the banks' lending terms had become more stringent, 35 per cent felt that they had become tighter and 24 per cent did not know.

The principal obstacles to raising external finance

The main problems mentioned by some respondents to raising external capital were:

■ *A reluctance on the part of the banks to lend capital without a demand for collateral;*

■ *Failure by the banks to appreciate the needs of business;*

■ *The risk averse nature of providers of capital in the UK; and*

■ *The paucity of venture capital – especially of small sums – available for entrepreneurs.*

Helping SMEs gain access to finance

According to respondents to the IoD's survey, the actions which the Government could take to help SMEs get access to finance are (in descending order of popularity):

■ *The provision of grants;*

■ *Improved access to the Loan Guarantee Scheme (now to be subsumed in the new Enterprise Fund);*

■ *The promotion of a wider range of finance options;*

■ *The provision of more information on sources of finance;*

■ *Encouraging a greater use of equity finance.*

Promoting the growth of SMEs

Reducing the rate of corporation tax and making the 40 per cent first year tax relief on plant and machinery permanent were regarded as very useful by 59 per cent and 53 per cent of respondents respectively. Conversely, only 5 per cent of respondents thought that the creation of eight new Institutes for Enterprise in universities would be a very useful development.

USEFUL CONTACTS

For further information on financing growth readers should first consult their professional advisers. The organisations listed below may be useful:

British Bankers Association
Tel: 020 7216 8800
Website: www.bba.org.uk

British Franchise Association
Tel: 01491 578049
Website: www.british-franchise.org.uk

British Venture Capital Association
Tel: 020 7240 3846
Website: www.bvca.co.uk

Business Links
Tel: 0345 567765
Website: www.businesslink.co.uk

Department for Education and Employment (DfEE)
Tel: 020 7925 5555
Website: www.dfee.gov.uk

Department of Trade and Industry
Tel: 020 7215 5000
Website: www.dti.gov.uk

Factors and Discounters Association (FDA)
Tel: 020 8332 9955
Website: www.factors.org.uk

Financing and Leasing Association
Tel: 020 7836 6511
Website: www.fla.org.uk

Grant Thornton
Tel: 020 7728 2758
Website: www.grant-thornton.co.uk

Institute of Credit Management (ICM)
Tel: 01780 722900
Website: www.icm.org.uk

Institute of Directors Information and Advisory Service
(IoD members only)
Tel: 020 7451 3100
Website: www.iod.co.uk